Why Am I Like This?

Why Am I Like This?

Dr. Jen Martin

Illustrated by
Holly Jolley

Princeton Architectural Press, New York

Contents

Who am I ?

What makes me tick?

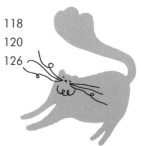

Questions to ask your brain

The human brain is 'the most complex object in the known universe', according to Professor of Neuroscience Christof Koch. This raises a conundrum: is the human brain capable of understanding itself? What really makes us tick, and will we ever truly understand what drives us to think, feel and act in certain ways?

People have been studying how the human brain works since the Ancient Greeks, over 2000 years ago. In their endeavor to understand the human mind and its functions, psychologists have asked many profound questions, such as "What is consciousness?"; "What determines personality?"; "Do we have free will?"; "Why do we dream?"; and "How do we learn?" These are fundamental questions for society and civilization, and our answers to them have changed enormously since Wilhelm Wundt opened the Institute of Experimental Psychology in 1879, marking the beginning of modern psychology. But alongside these fascinating existential questions, there are other things we don't yet understand: questions about the decisions, habits and experiences of everyday life that aren't always easy to explain.

Questions like, why do most of us continue to procrastinate, even when a major deadline is looming? Is it simply a bad habit, or can understanding what's going on inside our brains when we procrastinate help us to stop doing it? Why don't we all notice that even when we're awake, we spend roughly an hour and a half each day with our eyes closed? Why do we sometimes get songs stuck in our heads? And importantly: what's the best way to "unstick" a song that's stuck?

We've all asked ourselves questions like these and heard the accompanying urban myths and old wives' tales that attempt to explain them. It can be easy to assume these accepted wisdoms are true, but the fact is, many of the answers you've heard don't reflect our current scientific knowledge on the topics.

In thinking about such questions as a scientist, I often ask, "Has anyone ever properly researched that?" Happily, almost always, the answer is yes. These days, with the advent of so many research innovations and technologies, you'd be amazed at the kinds of questions researchers have begun to find answers to.

In this book I share the latest scientific research from psychology, neuroscience, sociology and other fields: the explanations researchers have arrived at in their quest to understand our brains and behavior better.

But while we have made huge advances in our understanding of the human brain over the past 150 years, there's still so much we don't fully understand. For example, it's still a mystery exactly how our brains process information. And we don't know how the movement of electrical and chemical signals between nerve cells in our brains results in us feeling pain or experiencing remorse or seeing the color blue.

In fact, in many ways we know more about the Earth and our place in the Universe than we know about our own brains: we have a pretty good idea of how life began and, although we can't go there, we are confident we know what the center of Earth looks like. We've explored and continued to study other planets and we've managed to send spacecraft beyond the edge of our solar system.

But the more we come to understand our own brains, the more questions we have about why we've evolved to be the way we are. Will the human brain ever manage to uncover all of its own secrets? Perhaps not, but that will never stop it from trying.

Who Am I ?

LET'S DELVE INTO YOUR MEMORIES,
THE SMELLS THAT MAKE YOU
HOMESICK, HOW MANY FRIENDS
YOU HAVE, AND HOW YOU'RE LIKELY
TO FEEL ON YOUR NEXT BIG BIRTHDAY.

Why can't I remember my childhood?

What's your earliest memory? Few people can remember anything from their childhoods earlier than age three. Despite some claiming otherwise, research suggests that people aren't able to remember their own births. Other research suggests we have trouble remembering events clearly before the age of seven.

Why can't we remember specific events from early in our lives? We certainly don't forget skills like walking, talking, and riding a bike we learn during those first few years.

One theory suggests childhood amnesia is a result of lack of language. If children don't have the necessary vocabulary to describe an event when it happens, they aren't able to describe it later, even after learning the necessary words.

Recent research suggests we forget our early years because at the time, so many new brain cells were being formed in the hippocampus, an important brain structure involved in memory formation. Essentially, the new brain nerve cells disrupt the circuits (and memories) that have already been formed in our brains. The period of time we can't remember may represent the time our brains were learning how to learn and remember.

THANKS FOR THE MEMORIES

There are a number of types of amnesia, some more common than others. Retrograde amnesia is when all memories formed before a particular event—such as a brain injury—are lost. Scientists have been fascinated by this kind of amnesia for more than 120 years and have studied many patients affected by it. In one case, a woman known as GH woke up after surgery performed in August 2002. She was convinced it was May 1989 and was unable to recognize her own children. GH simply couldn't remember anything about her life from May 1989 onward.

More recent research shows that the lost memories may in fact still be intact in the brain, but that access to the memories is blocked because of disease or trauma. The researchers found particular cells called Engram cells retained these memories, and that shining a light on the cells could recall them.

There are also a variety of more complex and unusual examples of amnesia. A professional cellist developed severe amnesia after suffering a viral infection of the brain. He was unable to recall any events from his past life or remember any of his friends or family. He also had difficulty forming new memories. But he could still remember and play every piece of music he had ever learned, sight-read new music, and learn music he had never heard before. This suggests that the areas of the brain responsible for learning and remembering music are separate to the areas of the brain involved with other kinds of memory.

JUST KEEP SWIMMING

There are plenty of movies that depict extreme cases of amnesia, some more scientifically accurate than others. Remember Dory in the movie *Finding Nemo*? And Leonard Shelby in *Memento*? These are two of the more accurate movie portrayals of amnesia—in both cases, the movies depict anterograde amnesia.

People suffering anterograde amnesia retain their identity and memories of their lives before a particular event (like a head injury) but completely lose the ability to form new memories. In *Memento*, Shelby is shown tattooing facts about his wife's murder onto his body as the only way to be able to hold onto them.

We understand stacks about this type of amnesia because of a famous patient known as Henry M. Henry, whose amnesia was the result of brain surgery performed to try to reduce his epileptic seizures. The surgery removed a number of areas of his brain tissue and left him with no memories of anything that happened to him after the surgery and the inability to retain any new information for more than a few minutes.

There is truth to the cliché that you never forget how to ride a bicycle.

Jennifer Talarico, Professor of Psychology, Lafayette College

In the movie *50 First Dates*, Drew Barrymore plays Lucy, a teacher who is only able to retain her memory over the course of each day. Each morning she wakes having no memory of previous days.

Similar to the fictional story of Lucy, a patient known as FL wasn't able to retain memories from one day to the next as the result of a car accident in 2005. During any one day her memory was normal, but her memory of each day disappeared after a night of sleep.

In a fascinating twist, subsequent research suggested her own experience of amnesia may have been unconsciously influenced by her knowledge of how amnesia had been depicted in the movie. When she didn't realize that she was being tested on something she had learned prior to that day, FL's memory was quite good. Drew Barrymore happened to be her favorite actress and with time and treatment, FL's amnesia improved.

A true case of life imitating art.

Why do I cringe at

Whether Myers-Briggs, the Big Five, or HEXACO, decades of research have gone into validating personality questionnaires, with millions of people taking these tests every year. The tests all attempt to do the same thing—characterize your personality according to some key traits. How extroverted are you? How conscientious? How neurotic? And the general consensus has long been that our personalities are pretty constant through time: once an extrovert, always an extrovert. But think back over your own life—do you feel like the same person now as you were in your teens? It turns out the idea we're stuck with certain personality traits for our whole lives may be wrong.

IN IT FOR THE LONG HAUL

To get an idea of how personality changes over time, we need to study people over many years. There have

been a few of these longitudinal personality studies, with the longest-running of them all lasting more than 60 years. The study started in 1947 when 1,208 14-year-old Scottish students were rated by their teachers on six personality traits: self-confidence, perseverance, stability of moods, conscientiousness, originality, and desire to excel. The ratings were put together into a single measure of dependability. Fast-forward 63 years, and 174 members of the original group agreed to take part in the study. They rated themselves on the same six traits and also asked a close relative or friend to do the same.

It is important to note that this is not the perfect study: it included only a small group of people and you can imagine the teachers might have been much better at scoring some traits than others. But it still gives us some insight

teenage me?

into how similar—or different—these people were at the ages of 14 and 77.

TURNING OVER A NEW LEAF

It's a fair bet you've changed your dress sense and taste in music since you were a teenager. But the Scottish research suggests you may have changed in other more profound ways, too. Over the six decades of the study, many of the participants changed so much that their former personalities were barely recognizable. There was some similarity between the teenagers and nearly 80-year-olds in terms of how conscientious and generally stable each person's moods were, but beyond that the older Scots had very little in common with their former selves.

Why were there such big changes? There are lots of things that can affect your personality: your job, where you live, becoming a parent, being in a relationship, and experiencing trauma, for example. And some changes simply happen over time. Other research involving more than 130,000 adults over 59 years showed we tend to become more agreeable, conscientious, and emotionally stable as we get older, with no clear difference between men and women in the rates we change. There's also good evidence we continue to mature well into adulthood.

Whether you like it or not, you're likely to turn over at least one new leaf during your life. Hopefully the fact you're also going to become more agreeable means you're going to like the person you become.

Why does my time pass so quickly?

We know our perceptions of time change as a result of all sorts of factors. For example, emotions can play a big role. When we feel rejected, or depressed, time seems to slow down. But when listening to music we like, time seems to go faster. When people are presented with different images on a screen for exactly the same amount of time, they perceive angry faces as lasting longer than neutral ones and pictures of spiders as lasting longer than those of butterflies. Experiments confirm that when we feel genuinely frightened, we also perceive time to pass slowly.

The way we experience a period of time in the moment can also be very different from how we perceive the same period of time in hindsight. One example of this is known as the vacation paradox: when we're on vacation, the days rush by. But once we're home and looking back on our time away, we feel like we were on vacation for a long time because we had so many new experiences.

Researchers have identified that regardless of age, the more time-pressured we feel, the more likely we perceive the days, weeks, and months as passing too fast. This is closely linked to a perception of not having enough time to do all the things we want to do and is true of people in a variety of Western cultures.

What's consistent across all cultures is that as we age, we share the feeling time is speeding up. Psychologists and philosophers have been trying to explain this phenomenon for at least 130 years.

Researchers have asked people of different ages how quickly they feel time has passed during the previous week, month, year, and decade. Over the shorter time-scales, people of different ages have similar perceptions of the speed of time passing. But the older the person, the more likely they are to say the last 10 years have passed quickly.

WHY DO WE FEEL LIKE TIME IS RACING AWAY FROM US?

Scientists have several different theories about why we feel time flies as we get older. One is called the "proportionality theory." This theory simply argues that a year seems to pass much faster when you are 40 than when you are four because it constitutes only one small fortieth of your life, rather than a whole quarter.

How can we stop that feeling of things going too fast, of missing out on our own lives? It comes back to learning new things.

Patricia Costello, Professor of Psychology, Walden University

Many theories have to do with how many novel experiences we have at different stages of life. The idea is the first time we experience something, our brains store lots of information about it. This results in our memories of an event being rich and dense. So, when thinking back to childhood experiences, our many vivid memories give the impression these memories must have formed over a very long time. As psychologist Claudia Hammond explains, "the reason we remember our youth so well is that it is a period when we have more new experiences than in our thirties or forties. It's a time for firsts—first sexual relationships, first jobs, first travel without parents, first experience of living away from home, the first time we get much real choice over the way we spend our days."

In contrast, when our days are somewhat indistinguishable from one another, when we are following the same daily routines (as is more common later in life), passages of time seem to go faster. As adults we generally have fewer new experiences that imprint on our minds.

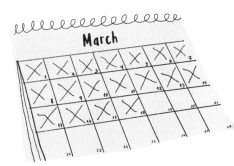

HOW CAN WE SLOW LIFE DOWN?

If you feel like life is escaping you and passing by far too fast for comfort, the answer may be to fill your time with new experiences. Going to new places and learning new things can very effectively slow down your internal sense of time. Anything that takes you out of your normal routine and introduces some novelty to your day should help to slow your perception of time passing. Research also suggests that making meaningful, noticeable progress toward your goals will also help expand your sense of time.

Slowing down and feeling under less time pressure could also help. A great solution is to take more vacations—a combination of reducing time pressure and maximizing new experiences. Although at the time a great vacation may seem to be over all too fast, as we look back we feel as though we've been away from the daily grind for a long time. A vacation in the name of research? Yes please.

Why do I get
so existential on

Whether you are 22, 28, 35, or 41 right now, your age probably doesn't have a strong influence on your life. But research shows that humans are very tuned in to real or perceived fresh starts when it comes to changing our habits. We know people are more likely to think about their health on Mondays. And people Google the term "diet" and

go to the gym much more often at the beginning of a week, month, or year, compared to at other times.

Ever made a New Year's Resolution? It turns out, birthdays act as strong landmarks for us, interrupting the otherwise trivial events that happen to us every day. So, it is no surprise that a birthday has the power to inspire changes in our behavior. Recent research into this topic focused on a few specific behaviors of people aged 25 to 64. The researchers were particularly interested in people they nicknamed the "9-enders"—people aged 29, 39, 49, and 59.

WHAT IS THE MEANING OF LIFE?

First the researchers considered results from the World Values Study. As part of this study, more than 42,000 people from across the world were asked how often they think about the meaning of life. Most people reported thinking about the meaning and purpose

IN THE YEAR BEFORE A MILESTONE BIRTHDAY, PEOPLE ARE MORE LIKELY TO REFLECT ON THEIR LIVES AND MAKE SIGNIFICANT CHANGES. WHY ARE WE SO AFFECTED BY THESE ESSENTIALLY ARBITRARY POINTS IN TIME?

some birthdays?

of their lives often, but 9-enders were found to consider these things significantly more often than people whose age ended in any other digit.

Contemplating whether your life has meaning results in either a positive or negative response depending on your conclusion. On the plus side, being a 9-ender makes it more likely you will run your first marathon. The researchers looked at the ages of 500 first-time marathon runners and 74 of them were 9-enders. That number is 48 percent more than we would expect if age had no relation to when people decide to run their first marathon. The researchers also looked at whether race times suggest 9-enders train harder than at other stages of their lives. And yes, runners aged 29 or 39 tended to finish about two percent faster at this age compared to the years before and after that birthday. This suggests they trained harder for the race in the year before they turned 30 or 40.

But the study also assessed the ages of more than eight million male users of an online dating site specifically designed for people seeking affairs. There were more than 950,000 men aged 29, 39, 49, or 59, which was nearly 18 percent more than would be expected by chance. (The pattern was also true for women, but the trend wasn't as strong.)

MAJOR BIRTHDAY, MAJOR DECISIONS
Why do these milestone birthdays have such an effect on our behavior? There are a number of theories. It may be the start of a new decade gives us distance from our past imperfections, providing inspiration to improve ourselves. It could also be that a significant birthday takes away our focus from the day-to-day minutiae of life and encourages us to think about the big picture. Whatever the reason, the message is clear: if you're a 9-ender, prepare to make some big decisions.

Why do some smells make me homesick?

Smells are complex. For example, the scent of chocolate is made up of hundreds of different odor molecules. Our noses have 1,000 smell receptors, which occur in a small area in the upper part of our nostrils' lining. These receptors detect odor molecules and send messages to the brain, resulting in us smelling a particular smell.

Early estimates put the number of different smells our noses could distinguish at around 10,000. But recent research upped the figure to one trillion different smells. And one trillion is an average—the range is 80 million to a thousand trillion unique scents for different people. These findings give your nose first prize for the most sensitive organ in your body in terms of the number of different inputs it can tell apart.

Why are our noses so sensitive? It's possible we evolved to be great at detecting smells for safety. Scientists suggest our sense of smell may have been just as important as language in giving us modern humans an evolutionary leg up. It was a distinct advantage for our ancestors to be able to smell fire, tasty but hard-to-find food, or food that had gone off.

Indeed, many women will tell you they knew they were pregnant way before any pregnancy test could confirm it because of their enhanced sense of smell. It makes sense we have evolved to be particularly good

at detecting food that could cause miscarriage. It's also been proposed morning sickness nausea is a result of this heightened sense of smell.

And in fact, without smell, we can't even taste food. Next time you are congested, notice how little taste your food has. Or try this simple experiment: pinch your nose shut with your fingers and eat a jellybean. It will taste a little sweet, but you won't be able to work out what flavor your jellybean was until you open your nose, swallow, and allow the smell to enter your nostrils.

WHY SMELLS EVOKE MEMORIES

Scientists call the involuntary experience of particular smells making us immediately recall childhood memories olfactory-evoked recall. The effect is also known as the Proust Effect after a description in Proust's *In Search of Lost Time* in which a character suddenly vividly recalls long-forgotten childhood memories while smelling a tea-soaked madeleine cookie.

The most common nostalgic smells are associated with baking bread and cakes, but other cooking smells are also common. And smells are not only good at evoking memories in general, they are particularly linked to emotional memories. Research has shown our memories are most emotional when triggered by scents, as opposed to sounds or images. Hence the heart-wrenching pangs of homesickness when you smell something that immediately transports you back home.

There are several theories as to why smell, memory, and emotion are so tightly linked. A major clue comes from the fact the olfactory bulb (the part of the brain responsible for processing information about smells) and the amygdala and hippocampus (regions of the brain associated with processing emotion and storing long-term memories respectively) are all located close to one another. Recent research even suggests some long-term memories might be stored in part of the olfactory bulb.

You smell something and you remember your grandmother's living room or your first day of school or your first lover...there's always a very strong emotional tinge to these memories.

Stuart Firestein, Professor of Neuroscience, Columbia University

Smells are connected to memories by networks of nerves in our brains and it has been shown when we smell something during an emotional experience, that smell is neurally woven together with the memory in the same region of the brain. Once the link has initially formed, a distinct smell has an amazing capacity to trigger the associated memory for many years to come.

PUTTING YOUR NOSE TO WORK

An exciting application of the fact we form clear memories linking smell and emotion is the possibility that smells could be used as evidence in criminal trials. The argument is that witnessing a crime is likely to be an extremely emotional event, and an eyewitness may be able to identify a criminal by their unique smell. Research so far suggests this approach has promise, but the body odor of the criminal may also get confused with other smells present at the scene.

While we wait to see if police lineups incorporate smell in the future, close your eyes and take a long, deep breath. How many different scents can you smell? How many of them can you put a name to? Marvel for a moment at the amazing capacity of your humble nose.

YOU'RE PROBABLY AWARE THAT TOO MUCH NOISE IS BAD FOR YOU. NOISE HAS BEEN SHOWN TO CAUSE STRESS, INSOMNIA, AND EVEN HEART DISEASE. IT'S TIME WE EMBRACED THE POWER OF SILENCE.

Why does silence calm me?

The word "noise" comes from the Latin "nausea," meaning pain or queasiness. And noise, now often referred to as noise pollution, has been blamed for a variety of ills. Sleeping problems, high blood pressure, difficulty concentrating, and heart disease are some of the main concerns. And noise can also simply be irritating, hence the diagnosis of "noise annoyance." Sound vibrates the bones in our ears, which get converted into electrical signals to our brain. Our bodies respond to these signals, often resulting in the release of stress hormones like cortisol. Noise has this effect even if you're sound asleep, and it's not good news. If you live in a noisy place, you're probably also living with permanently high levels of stress. Kids living in noisy places may experience learning difficulties among other problems. What to do about it? Research suggests it's not enough to simply seek a little peace and quiet, but that silence is more powerful than we ever guessed.

OF MICE, MEMORIES, AND MUSIC
Ten years ago, some scientists who were also amateur musicians wanted to study how music affects people physiologically. Study participants listened to a two minute track of each of six different music styles, with a two minute

> *Noise—even at levels that do not produce any hearing damage—causes stress and is harmful to humans.*
>
> Gary Evans, Professor of Human Ecology, Cornell College

break between each track. The researchers measured breathing rate, blood pressure, and various other physiological changes. They were expecting to find the tempo, rhythm, and melody of the music, as well as people's previous musical training and own musical preferences to have an effect. And they did find these things. But the biggest finding of the study was something the researchers didn't even set out to look at: it was the two minutes of silence between tracks that had the biggest relaxation effect.

More recently, researchers studied the effects of various sounds on the brains of adult mice. The sounds of interest were music, baby mouse calls, and white noise. Silence was used as a control for the experiment. Again, without trying to, this study showed the power of silence: none of the actual sounds had a long-term effect on the brain. But two hours of silence a day had a profound effect on the mice's brains: they developed new brain cells in the hippocampus, an area of the brain responsible for emotions and memory.

QUIETING THE MIND

At some level we all know quiet is good for us. Sales of noise-canceling headphones have skyrocketed in recent years and Finland's Tourist Board's slogan "Silence, Please" has been a massively successful way to market the country to the world. Most of us know time in nature will do us a world of good and this is at least partly due to the quiet that can often be found in natural places.

Your brain is always active, but when it's not distracted by noise, or being required to focus on a particular task, it enters a state called the "default mode of brain function." This is when our brains get to do a bit of housekeeping: processing messages that come both from the outside world and from within ourselves. In silence, our brain has the opportunity to integrate these messages. We can reflect on who we are, empathize with others, reflect on our own well-being, and think creatively. Silence allows us to connect with ourselves and replenishes our inner reserves.

TOO MUCH OF A GOOD THING?

So, does all this mean the more silence, the better? Not so fast. The most silent place on Earth, an anechoic chamber in Minnesota, is so quiet that the background noise is measured as a negative. This means you can hear your heartbeat, your stomach gurgle, and sometimes even your nerves firing. It's a place companies can test the volume of their products and where NASA can send astronauts to get a taste of the silence of space.

But if you think it would be a great place to hang out and grow some new brain cells, you're wrong. Most people find the room deeply disorientating. Reports are that the longest anyone has even been able to cope with staying in the room is 45 minutes.

Finland sounds better, thanks.

Why do horror movies give

A recent study in Denmark fitted participants with heart rate monitors before they entered a haunted house. The attraction included actors in costume playing a variety of characters. After they left the house, the volunteers gave an overall rating of how scared they had been and how much they had enjoyed the experience. They also rated their fear and enjoyment at a few specific locations in the house: for example, when a zombie jumped out from behind a staircase and someone covered in blood ran straight toward them wielding a chainsaw.

The relationship between fear and enjoyment for the haunted house visitors suggest we're a bit like Goldilocks. The more scared we are, the more we like it…but only to a point. When our hearts start to race but quickly return to normal, that's enjoyment. But when our heart rate goes up and stays up, it's

a signal we're no longer having fun. We like our scary experiences not too terrifying, not too lame; they have to be just right.

I'M NOT SCARED, YOU'RE SCARED

Why do we stop having fun when we feel too terrified? Research suggests it all comes down to context. Imagine you're at home, cozy on your couch and watching a horror movie. You know you're in a safe place, and despite getting caught up in the suspense of it all, you know the movie is fictional, and your fear feels exciting.

Imagine you get so caught up in the movie that you forget it's not real. You no longer feel safe and suddenly movie night has taken a dark turn. Why? Because different parts of your brain are active during different fear experiences. When you're scared your amygdala—an important part of your

me a thrill?

brain's emotional center—activates, your blood pressure and heart rate rise and you start breathing quickly. You become hyper-alert to what is going on around you: this is the "fight or flight" response.

Other parts of your brain (your hippocampus and frontal cortex, for example) get involved to help you work out whether or not the threat is real. Imagine you're swimming in the ocean and you see a shark's fin. Chances are you're going to experience a major fear response. See the same animal at an aquarium and the thinking part of your brain tells the emotional part of your brain that you're OK. Context is everything: now you're just blown away by how incredible sharks are.

WHY DO WE ENJOY (SOME) FEAR?
What is it about overcoming a fear response that feels good? You feel very alive when you're terrified, largely because you're fully focused on one thing. And once your brain decides the chainsaw-wielding actor isn't a real threat, you can relabel the experience as a thrill that doesn't happen every day. As a result, you feel in control, safe, and, importantly, more confident in your ability to confront something scary next time. You get a self-esteem boost simply from having survived.

WILL WEARING RED MAKE YOU MORE ATTRACTIVE?

DO SPORTS TEAMS DRESSED IN BLACK PLAY MORE AGGRESSIVELY?

ARE GOOD GUYS IN MOVIES OFTEN DRESSED IN WHITE?

Why do colors change my mood?

In a variety of animals, red symbolizes attraction. For example, many female primates display red coloration on their faces or private parts to signal to males they are fertile and ready to mate. It's not so different among humans. Men sit closer to women wearing red and ask more intimate questions of them. And men perceive women dressed in red as both sexually receptive and attractive. Male diners even give bigger tips to waitresses wearing red rather than white.

And women aren't immune to the allure of red. Researchers showed women headshots of men and asked them their first impression of the person, without mentioning color or gender. Half of the women were shown the man against a red background and the other half the same picture, but against a white background. Women rank a man shown against red consistently more attractive than the same man against white.

A man seen with red will also be rated as high in social status and with a higher potential for success. The same was true for men wearing red, rather than white, clothing.

The research is clear: at a subconscious level, red acts as a sexual attraction booster for both sexes.

THE POWER OF COLOR

Color can have huge effects on our perceptions, and the associations we have with different colors have been the focus of much research. It goes far beyond just "red is sexy." We also know that wearing red enhances performance in a variety of sports. And when you see red, your physical reactions become both faster and stronger. But red can also signal danger and potentially cause stress. Researchers tested the effect of the color red on the way kids performed in tests: when the cover of an IQ test booklet was red, the kids performed less well.

Other colors change our behavior too. Professional ice hockey players are more aggressive when wearing black, rather than white uniforms. We assume that people dressed in white are likely to be good, whereas those dressed in black are bad. *Star Wars*, anyone?

When you see the color pink, your muscles relax. In the 1970s, Alexander Schauss, a biosocial researcher, even argued that painting prison cells pink would reduce aggressive and violent incidents. The opponents' locker room at the University of Iowa has been painted pink since 1979. This fact has been used to explain the home team's success on the football field.

SHOW ME THE MONEY

Color is serious business to marketers. Research shows that visual appearance is overwhelmingly important to consumers choosing what to buy, and up to 90 percent of a person's impression of what an object looks like is based on color. So, it's not surprising that packaging designers are absolute experts when it comes to color associations.

These days, the color green has become synonymous with natural, healthy, and good. You can find it adorning packaging for everything from beer to sugary yogurt, but it's also the predominant color used in organic food packaging. In 2000, Heinz carried out a marketing experiment and created a green-packaged tomato sauce, which was incredibly lucrative (but no less sugar-laden). We may think we're too smart to be fooled by simple marketing tricks, but this study suggests otherwise.

And the green message can be far more subtle. Researchers asked volunteers to imagine they were standing in line at a supermarket checkout, feeling hungry and had candy bars in front of them. The people were then shown an image of a candy bar with either a green or red nutrition label. They were otherwise identical; in both cases, the label stated that the candy bar contained 260 calories.

We typically think of color in terms of beauty and aesthetics. But color carries meaning as well, and affects our perception and behavior in important ways without our awareness.

Andrew Elliot, Professor of Psychology, University of Rochester

The result is not a surprise: people thought the bar with the green label was healthier. The researchers then showed people pictures of identical candy bars, but with either a white or green calorie label. Again, green signaled healthy. The more that healthy eating habits mattered to the study volunteer, the more they believed the bar with the green label was the healthier option. Color is a force to be reckoned with.

DO YOU ENJOY THE PEACE AND QUIET OF YOUR OWN THOUGHTS? OR DO YOU DESPERATELY SEEK DISTRACTION? MANY OF US WILL GO TO GREAT LENGTHS TO AVOID SIMPLY HAVING TO THINK BY OURSELVES.

Why do I hate doing

It sounds like a very simple exercise. All you need to do is sit alone in an empty room for six to fifteen minutes, and you must stay awake and in your chair. Easy, right? Psychologists from the University of Virginia and Harvard did this exercise multiple times with a variety of people spanning ages 18–77 years of age and found the same thing: people don't like doing nothing.

More than half of the study participants rated the experience as somewhat or more than somewhat difficult. Nearly half admitted to not enjoying the experience much. They found the exercise far less enjoyable than reading magazines, doing crosswords, or listening to music. Results for two people had to be dumped from the study because in one case the researcher left a pen in the lab by mistake and the person used it to write a to-do list. Another time an instruction sheet was left in the room and the study participant used it to practice origami.

The next step in the study was to give people specific topics to think about, like planning a vacation. But even that didn't help people to enjoy the experience any more.

WE ALL HATE DOING NOTHING

The people who took part in this research didn't like spending even brief periods of time alone in a room with nothing to do but think or daydream. It seems we are desperate for distractions. But would people prefer an unpleasant activity over no activity at all? Was the experience of time with no external distractions so bad that people would avoid it by inflicting pain on

absolutely nothing?

themselves? You've already guessed the answer. For some people, yes.

At the start of the next study, participants were given a mild electric shock. When asked if the shock was bad enough that they would be willing to pay to avoid being shocked again, 75 percent said yes. But when those people were left alone in a room for 15 minutes without distraction, 67 percent of men and 25 percent of women gave themselves electric shocks as a distraction from simply being alone with their thoughts. On average people gave themselves one to two shocks, but one man pressed the button 190 times. Participants simply preferred an electric shock over boredom.

WHY IS IT SO HARD TO GO WITHOUT DISTRACTION?

The psychologists running the study admitted that they expected people to find it easy to amuse themselves: we have big brains full of memories and the ability to reflect on the past, plan for the future, and create imaginary worlds. But that clearly wasn't that case. According to Professor Timothy D. Wilson: "I think [our] mind is built to engage in the world. So when we don't give it anything to focus on, it's kind of hard to know what to do. I suppose it's kind of circular. We wouldn't crave these things if we weren't in need of distractions. But having so many available keeps us from learning how to disengage."

Can we lay the blame firmly at the feet of social media? Probably not. Study participants who used social media less often were no better at daydreaming. Enjoyment of time alone wasn't related to social media or smartphone use, or age. Interestingly, though, Wilson and colleagues did find a small correlation between meditation experience and the ability to be happily alone with thoughts. Time to practice your lotus pose?

Why do I find baby animals so cute?

Baby animals, in particular mammals, rank high in the cuteness stakes. When twin baby pandas were born at the National Zoo in Washington, D.C., 868,000 people watched Panda Cam over one weekend. There are more "cute baby animal" websites than you could ever have time to look at, and Buzzfeed even attempted a definitive ranking of the cutest baby animals. In case you're wondering, baby otters beat puppies, kittens, and panda cubs to claim ultimate cuteness.

Unsurprisingly, there's money to be made out of cuteness: advertisements featuring cute children or animals abound. Cute soft toys are a massive industry and we can trace how these soft toys have become cuter over time. During the twentieth century for example, the humble teddy bear changed from having a long snout to bearing a short snout and high forehead. Similarly, Mickey Mouse changed over a 50-year period—ending up with a larger relative head and far bigger eyes. These days, it's hard to think of a Disney or Pixar character that doesn't have enormous eyes, from mermaids, princesses, fish, ants, monsters, and emotions to cars, the eyes are gigantic.

Whether you're talking anime, manga, or Pokémon, popular Japanese characters also tend to have exaggerated features, in particular, large eyes.

Japan has taken the worship of cute to a whole new level. Ever since Hello Kitty said her first hello in 1974, Kawaii (translated these days simply as cute, lovable, or adorable) has become a mainstay of Japanese popular culture. But what defines cute?

BABY FACE

It's not just huge eyes that cute things share. There are a number of other features we associate with cute: a large head (Hello Kitty's head accounts for half her body), a small "button" nose, chubby cheeks, and a prominent forehead. Research across cultures and races has shown this combination of characteristics is considered near universally adorable. Why have we evolved to respond so strongly to this set of facial features? Because these are the features of human babies.

Filling in an emotional need is exactly where kawaii plays a significant role.

Christine Yano, Professor of Anthropology, University of Hawaii

Back in 1943, Konrad Lorenz dubbed this set of features the baby schema. Research in the 1970s showed we rate babies with a more pronounced set of these features most attractive, that we like to look at cute babies, and that babies make us smile. Lorenz argued that these physical features have come to signify vulnerability and prompt our parental instincts.

Essentially, we are hardwired to want to nurture cute things. It makes sense: if we hadn't evolved to be compelled to take care of our completely helpless newborn babies, humans probably wouldn't have lasted long. Interestingly, although men and women are equally good at picking the age of babies, and how happy they look, women are much better at rating different levels of cuteness, according to standard "cuteness features" including the nose, cheeks, and forehead. And you don't have to be a parent to feel this overwhelming desire to take care of a cute baby.

Recent research recorded what was going on in the brains of women who had no children as they looked at photos of cute babies and found that photos activated parts of the brain involved with our reward centers: we really are primed to respond to cute.

CARE, CONCENTRATION...AND BUBBLE WRAP

Seeing something cute doesn't just make us want to care for a baby. We know looking at cute things makes us feel more positive: research has found that watching cats online makes you happier. And research has also shown that looking at cute images makes us pay more attention to detail, narrow our focus, and behave more carefully. Yes, that's right—checking out cute pictures on Instagram can improve your concentration and may even make you work more productively.

But contrary to what you might expect, cute things can also make us feel aggressive. Have you ever had the urge to pinch the chubby cheeks of a cute baby? Squeeze a kitten within an inch of its life? Given that cute things are often vulnerable, or fragile in some way, it seems odd they can lead us to say "you're so cute I want to gobble you up!" Researchers suggest the aggression results from frustration: we can't satisfy our intense desire to care for the cute thing in front of us, leading to an aggressive response. And just in case you're wondering, yes, scientists have carried out the ultimate experiment. Looking at adorably cute pictures also makes us pop more bubbles on a sheet of bubble wrap.

Why do I always feel

A recent study defined FOMO as "the uneasy and sometimes all-consuming feeling that you're missing out—that your peers are doing, in the know about, or in possession of more or something better than you." Sound familiar? Many people have written about their experience of FOMO and according to one survey, a quarter of adults and half of teenagers experience it. Recent research found people of all ages can experience FOMO and that it's associated with loneliness, low self-compassion, and low self-esteem. It also often accompanies feelings of incompetence, as well as low levels of autonomy and connection with other people. With FOMO comes

anxiety, restlessness, and feelings of inadequacy. FOMO leads us to want to constantly know what is going on in other places. And since the rise of social media, checking in on other people is something we can do instantly, 24 hours a day, seven days a week.

IS THE GRASS ON FACEBOOK GREENER?

It's hard to imagine a world without social media. On average, we interact with our phones more than 2,500 times a day. We know people who experience high levels of FOMO are also more likely to use social media.

Why? Social media makes us more likely to compare our lives and our achievements with other people. And it's not a fair comparison: we know our own lives in messy warts-and-all detail. But our view of the lives of people we interact with only online is like a highlights reel: carefully edited and curated.

DO YOU EVER FEEL LEFT OUT? THAT EVERYONE ELSE IS SOMEWHERE MORE EXCITING THAN YOU, EXPERIENCING THINGS FAR MORE INTERESTING THAN YOU? THAT'S FEAR OF MISSING OUT, OTHERWISE KNOWN AS FOMO.

like I'm missing out?

FOMO'S ANCIENT BEGINNING

It's tempting to think FOMO is a very recent phenomenon, but we've probably always experienced it to some degree—social media has simply upped the ante. In times gone by, our survival depended on the fact we were social. It was vital we were aware of potential threats, both to ourselves and our tribe; being "in the loop" was essential. We needed to know where to catch and grow food, who was sick, and who could help in any given situation. We evolved to keep tabs on the people around us. The problem is simple: we are now trying to keep tabs on too many people, and we don't have a realistic view of their lives.

There are two common responses to FOMO: one is to commit to every opportunity, the other is to commit to none. Saying yes to everything results in overwhelm and a schedule that is impossible to keep up with. But never saying yes (generally in an attempt to keep all options open) is equally problematic, potentially resulting in a person doing nothing for fear that any choice will be the wrong choice. We end up in a physiologically stressed state trying to stay on top of everything we might be missing out on.

What can we do to tackle FOMO? The answers aren't rocket science. We need to turn off our phones, be more aware of the fantasy social media can easily portray, and pay attention to whatever is going on around us. After all, the only thing we really miss out on when FOMO takes hold is our own lives. And these days many more people are embracing JOMO—the joy of missing out.

Why do I feel like I'm being watched?

They say the eyes are the windows to the soul: eye contact is one of the most powerful forms of human communication. Unlike all other primates, human eyes make it extremely obvious which direction we are looking: the exposed white area around the colored iris gives it away, even from a distance. In most other animals, the iris takes up almost all of the eye, or the area around the iris is darker. Either way, it's very hard to tell which direction animal eyes are looking, which probably evolved as a way for predators to hide the direction of their gaze from potential prey.

From their very first days, babies prefer faces looking directly at them. And from an early age, our brains respond more to a face looking directly into our eyes than one looking away (see page 96). We have a "gaze detection" system—a network of nerves in our brains sensitive to whether someone is looking right at us, or just past us. Researchers suggest we have evolved to be so tuned into the direct gaze of other people because it forms the basis of human cooperation and social behavior.

SIXTH SENSE?

But what about the feeling of being watched? According to surveys, up to 94 percent of people report having experienced the feeling of being stared

at, only to look up and discover it was true. If you've had the experience, you'll know it can feel like extrasensory perception, or a sixth sense. The phenomenon has also been the subject of plenty of research, going back at least as early as 1898.

Early studies dismissed the idea, declaring that the feeling of being watched was simply a result of being nervous about what may be going on behind your back. There are also other straightforward possible explanations. It could be that in your peripheral vision, you've noticed the telltale signs of someone looking in your direction. We are very sensitive to body language; if someone's body is facing away from us, but their head points toward us, it's an immediate giveaway they may be looking at us. At the very least, it makes us look up to get more information.

It may also be a self-fulfilling prophecy: if you're nervous someone is watching you, you may start fidgeting. Your movement alone will make it more likely someone will indeed look at you. There's also the possibility that as you sit on the train feeling like you're being watched, the very act of you looking up from your phone makes the person opposite you look up too. When your eyes meet, you wrongly assume this person has been looking at you all along. Research has shown we are hardwired to assume other people are looking at us, even if they're not. The argument suggests that we evolved to think this way because it keeps us alert to danger and ready to interact.

But there's also a far more intriguing possibility: perhaps your brain has detected someone else's gaze without your eyes seeing a thing.

YOUR BRAIN IS WATCHING

The evidence for this somewhat unnerving idea comes from studies involving people who have lost their visual cortex due to brain injury. The visual cortex is the part of your brain that processes visual information and maps your view of the world. One fascinating study reported the experiences of a man who is "cortically blind." Although his eyes are fully functional, and send information to the brain, his visual cortex was damaged by two strokes. As a result, he doesn't have what we traditionally think of as sight. But what do our eyes take in beyond what our sight shows us? Quite a lot. Scientists call this extremely rare condition blindsight.

Although this man (known as TN) can't see, researchers showed him pictures of faces, some looking right at him, some looking away. At the same time, they measured activity in his amygdala—the part of the brain in charge of facial recognition and emotions. Even though TN couldn't consciously see the pictures and said he couldn't tell the difference, there was more activity in his amygdala when he was presented with a face looking directly at him. His brain knew when someone was looking right at him, even when he couldn't actually see the face.

Judging if others are looking at us may come naturally, but it's actually not that simple. Our brains have to do a lot of work behind the scenes.

Colin Clifford, Professor of Psychology, University of New South Wales

The eyes of a person with blindsight still receive light, and that light is converted to information that makes its way through nerve pathways in the brain to the visual cortex. But because this part of the brain is damaged, the information can't be properly processed. As a result, a person with blindsight doesn't consciously see anything, but that doesn't keep other parts of the brain's visual system from registering and responding to what is being taken in by the eyes.

What an extraordinary trick our brains are capable of. It may be that as long as a person looking at us is within our broad field of view, we can sense their eyes on us, without actually seeing them at all. This could explain the creepy feeling of being watched.

Why does everyone I know

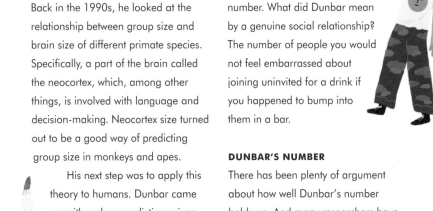

Evolutionary psychologist Robin Dunbar has spent 50 years studying primates. Back in the 1990s, he looked at the relationship between group size and brain size of different primate species. Specifically, a part of the brain called the neocortex, which, among other things, is involved with language and decision-making. Neocortex size turned out to be a good way of predicting group size in monkeys and apes.

His next step was to apply this theory to humans. Dunbar came up with a clear prediction: given the size of our neocortex, at any one time, we should only be able to maintain genuine social relationships with around 150 people. According to Dunbar, we simply don't have the brain space— or time—to nurture social relationships with more people than that. This prediction

of 150 relationships has become known as Dunbar's number. What did Dunbar mean by a genuine social relationship? The number of people you would not feel embarrassed about joining uninvited for a drink if you happened to bump into them in a bar.

DUNBAR'S NUMBER

There has been plenty of argument about how well Dunbar's number holds up. And many researchers have criticized different aspects of Dunbar's theory. But Dunbar's number does hold true in some situations. Many traditional hunter-gatherer societies are around the 150-people mark and a UK study found, on average, people sent 120–150 Christmas cards.

More recent research suggests that rather than thinking about our friends

have more friends than me?

in terms of a number, we should think about Dunbar's layers. Most of us have around five intimate friends, including a romantic partner if we have one, and 15 best friends. Going out in layers, we have 150 friends, 500 acquaintances, and a total of 1,500 people we can name if we see them.

ENTER SOCIAL NETWORKING

It's easy to imagine social networking sites have changed the landscape when it comes to how many friends we can have. We can broadcast our news to hundreds or thousands of people in an instant. We can stay up-to-date with the lives of as many people as we have scrolling time for. But a study of 450 undergraduate students found that although many of them had 300 or more Facebook friends, they

only considered an average of 75 of them as real friends.

A 2016 study asked more than 3,000 people for more detail about their Facebook friends. On average, these people had between 150 and 200 Facebook friends. But when asked how many of those people each could turn to in a crisis, the answer was four. How many would offer genuine sympathy in a difficult situation? Fourteen.

The quality of our relationships is directly related to how much time we invest in them and we simply don't have time to invest in hundreds of friendships. So next time you're about to open Facebook, maybe it would be better to give a friend a call instead.

Why do I feel like I'm going to be found out?

In 1978, psychologists Pauline Rose Clance and Suzanne Imes described a phenomenon among high-achieving women: imposter syndrome. Five years of research had highlighted how many successful women believed their success could be attributed to luck, chance, or errors in selection processes. These women were sure their abilities had been overestimated. Clance went on to create a scale to quantify the experience of imposter syndrome. Researchers have been studying the imposter syndrome ever since and we now know a lot about it. Despite the fact the imposter syndrome was first described in women, we now know men are just as likely to experience it. One study among university academics (a profession in which the imposter syndrome is rife) found men were even more likely than women to experience imposter syndrome.

Research suggests 70 percent of people will experience feelings of being an imposter at some point in their lives. And it's worth pointing out this phenomenon doesn't qualify as a syndrome according to the medical definition. According to Clance, if she could go back, she would call it the Imposter Experience since nearly everyone experiences it and it's not a mental illness.

People who don't feel like imposters are no more intelligent or competent or capable than the rest of us. It's very good news, because it means we just have to learn to think like non-imposters.

Dr. Valerie Young, author and imposter syndrome expert

COME ONE, COME ALL

An important aspect of the imposter syndrome is the fact each of us tends to think we are the only one suffering from it. We listen to the monologue of self-doubt going on in our own heads and mistakenly assume it's just us. But the truth is most people feel this way at least some of the time. When Olivia Fox Cabane asks incoming students at the notoriously highly-selective Harvard Business School each year: "How many of you in here feel that you are the one mistake the admissions committee made?" two-thirds of the students put up their hand. (And of course, it's somewhat terrifying to consider the possibility everyone around us is just winging it. We like to think the people out there flying planes, performing surgery, making decisions in court, and running our governments are highly competent.)

There are several common features among people experiencing imposter syndrome. The vast majority of "imposters" are able to successfully fulfill their work requirements despite their perceptions of incompetency. In fact, many "imposters" are high achievers who fail to internalize their success. Despite ample objective evidence of their achievements, "imposters" still feel like they are making it up as they go along and fear they are about to be unmasked.

Other features of imposter syndrome are a fear of failure; a tendency to attribute success to luck, error, or charm; and the feeling of having given others a false impression. People experiencing imposter syndrome may be perfectionists, but they may also fall victim to procrastination and often experience anxiety. "Imposters" often feel they need to stand out and be the very best compared with their peers. Interestingly, people suffering imposter syndrome crave praise and acknowledgment but feel uncomfortable when they receive it (because they don't think they deserve it).

Although men and women experience imposter syndrome in equal numbers, they do respond to it differently: women commonly work harder to try and prove themselves whereas men tend to avoid situations in which their weaknesses might be exposed.

FAKE IT 'TIL YOU MAKE IT

The most common advice we hear about how to deal with feelings of inadequacy is to "fake it 'til you make it." Pretend you feel confident and assured and ignore the nagging doubts. It's not bad advice, but we may be waiting for a long time to feel like we've "made it." The frustrating irony of imposter syndrome is the more experienced and senior you become, the more likely you are to find yourself being required to do new things, and therefore feeling like you are winging it. Getting better at your job isn't a guaranteed way of making your imposter syndrome go away.

There is plenty of other advice for coping with imposter syndrome. For example, practice accepting compliments, talk with the people around you about how you feel, and remember that feeling like a fraud is completely normal. It can also be useful to focus on what you're learning, rather than how you're performing. This is mindset theory: if you focus on how you're performing, you see any mistakes you make as evidence of your inadequacy. But if you have a growth mindset, your mistakes are simply part of the inevitable learning process.

And if all else fails, take heart from the words of UCLA Professor Jessica Collett, an expert in the field: "Imposterism is most often found among extremely talented and capable individuals, not people who are true imposters."

Why am I not a master of anything?

In 1993, Swedish psychologist Anders Ericsson and his colleagues investigated the practice habits of violin players undertaking training at the elite West Berlin Music Academy. They wanted to understand what made a brilliant violinist as opposed to a "very good" one. Their conclusion: you don't get to be a virtuoso with less than ten years of practice under your belt. And the more you practice, the better you are likely to be.

THE MAGIC NUMBER

So where did 10,000 hours come from? In Ericsson's study, by age 20, the best violinists had spent on average 10,000 hours studying violin. In contrast, the very good violinists had averaged only 7,800 hours of practice. Fast forward to 2008, and Malcolm Gladwell published his book *Outliers*. Gladwell wanted to know why standouts like Bill Gates and The Beatles were so successful. The key? According to Gladwell, 10,000 hours of practice. For example, The Beatles played thousands of live shows in Hamburg between 1960 and 1964, resulting in more than 10,000 hours of performance by the time they returned to England. With that, the "10,000-hour rule" took on a life of its own. Soon, 10,000 hours of practice became a rule-of-thumb; a magical threshold. How hard is it to reach the threshold? Four hours of practice, five days a week for ten years will get you there.

But research has slammed the 10,000-hour rule—unsurprisingly, the path to mastery is not quite so simple. For a start, the simple rule ignores the fact there are many forms of practice. Simply doing something over and over again for 10,000 hours doesn't guarantee you anything—except perhaps boredom. What's needed is not just accumulated hours, but a commitment to what's called "deliberate practice." Deliberate practice involves getting expert advice: having someone who can give you feedback and correct your mistakes.

And there's no evidence for a one-size-fits-all recipe for success. Back to the original study of violinists: 10,000 hours was not an exact number of hours reached, but rather an average of the time these top students spent practicing. It turns out some had practiced for far less than 10,000 hours. Others had accumulated more than 25,000 hours of practice.

in performance. And when the researchers looked solely at elite sportspeople, practice could only explain one percent of the differences in success. Another study found practice could explain about one-third of the differences in success among musicians and chess players.

Practice, although important, is nowhere near the whole story. Things like genes, personality, access to expert advice (as well as how good someone is at taking on feedback) must all be hugely influential too. The 10,000-hour rule has been debunked.

IF NOT PRACTICE, THEN WHAT?

Researchers have now pooled together the results of many studies in order to understand what role practice plays in mastery. For example, research published in 2016 explored the link between deliberate practice and performance across many different sports and found training accounted for only 18 percent of the variance

Why do I remember things that never happened?

It's not surprising our recollections of past events can be hazy. For example, seven weeks after the event, a researcher asked people about their memories of September 11, 2001. Among other questions, was "on September 11, did you see the videotape on television of the first plane striking the first tower?" Seventy-five percent of those asked were confident they remembered watching the footage on that day. Seems reasonable, except that the footage wasn't actually aired until a day later. A tiny detail, but a good illustration of the way we misremember events.

Research has shown we constantly fill in the gaps between real pieces of memory, and along the way we make assumptions, and plenty of mistakes. We construct our memories, without even being aware we're doing it. Emotional memories may be more accurate, but no memories are immune to contamination. Memories that are not quite right might lead to arguments and won't serve us well at trivia nights. But at least our memories always vaguely resemble the truth. Right? Wrong!

HOW WAS YOUR BALLOON RIDE?

Far more unsettling than misremembering some aspects of a real-life event is remembering an event that never took place. Researchers now

know how to implant a false memory. It turns out to be an easy-to-follow recipe, particularly successful when applied to people who are "prone to suggestion." What false memories can you implant? Unsurprisingly, it's easy to lead people to "recall" small, made-up details about a real event they witnessed. Most of us struggle to recall the small details of our lives anyway!

But under the right circumstances, it's possible to lead people to create wholly fake memories. Psychologists showed people doctored photos of themselves in a hot-air balloon. They followed up with a guided imagery exercise and voila! Half of the study participants had memories of the fictitious balloon ride. Researchers also successfully got people to remember they had accidentally spilled a bowl of punch on the parents of the bride at a wedding reception, despite the fact it never happened.

Participants in another study were asked to recall as many details as they could about a childhood event that was entirely made up, involving being lost at the mall. About 30 percent of the study participants later recalled being lost, some creating specific details about a kind adult who had helped them. Recollections of the fake event were less detailed than those of real events but nonetheless, these people were convinced the event had happened.

DID YOU COMMIT THE CRIME? (ARE YOU SURE?)

Can you imagine ever confessing to a crime you didn't commit? Seems unlikely, but research has shown how easily it can happen. In one experiment, people were falsely accused of making a computer crash by pressing the wrong key during a study supposedly about reaction times. All of those accused were completely innocent. Initially, all denied the charge. But after a witness admitted to having seen it happen, many signed a confession, felt guilty, and went on to form their own memories of the "crime."

In another study, 70 percent of people became convinced that as teenagers, they had committed an assault with a weapon, which led to an encounter with the police. Half of these recounted specifics of their dealings with the police. A little bit of suggestion from someone with authority goes a long way.

The question isn't whether our memories are false, it's how false are our memories.

Dr. Julia Shaw, Psychologist, University College London

And of course, witnesses aren't immune to false memories. In a series of experiments back in the 1970s, students were shown images depicting an accident between a car and a pedestrian. These students were then exposed to further information about the accident: either true (the car had been at a stop sign), or misleading (the car had been at a yield intersection). The results showed witnesses integrated this additional information into their memory of the event. Those who had been given the latter suggestion tended to claim they'd been at a yield intersection.

Given how powerful confessions are, what does all this mean for our legal system? Plenty. In particular, that the questioning of suspects (and witnesses) must be done very, very carefully.

WILL THE REAL MEMORY PLEASE RAISE ITS HAND?

How can you tell the difference between real and false memories? With great difficulty. Because once they've taken hold in your brain, false memories and real memories are pretty much indistinguishable.

What Makes Me Tick?

LET'S EXPLORE YOUR HABITS, FROM DRINKING COFFEE AND CRAVING JUNK FOOD AT NIGHT TO DOODLING WHEN YOU'RE IN A MEETING AND TAKING HUNDREDS OF PHOTOS

WE ALL KNOW THE SAYING "THE EARLY BIRD CATCHES THE WORM."

BUT ARE THERE ANY REAL BENEFITS TO BEING A MORNING PERSON?

WHAT DETERMINES WHETHER YOU'RE AN EARLY BIRD OR A NIGHT OWL ANYWAY?

Why do I keep pressing snooze?

Your body has an internal clock. It's located in the base of your brain, in the hypothalamus. You've probably heard the term "circadian rhythm": this is the natural sleep and wake cycle of all animals and is synced to the Earth's 24-hour cycle.

Unlike nocturnal animals, people are generally awake during the day. But there are differences in when we prefer to sleep. Your preferred sleep and wake times are your chronotype. Most people start their lives as early birds—many of us have personally experienced how early babies tend to wake up. But wake times usually shift later as we age, with teens notorious for their late nights and long sleep-ins.

Known as the sentinel hypothesis, the theory goes that a tribe of humans with staggered sleep schedules were at an evolutionary advantage: there was always someone wide awake and ready to stand guard. Today, some of us are early risers, some of us late risers, and many fall somewhere in between.

ALL IN THE GENES?

We've long known genes play a role in determining chronotypes, but recent research makes clear how complex the link is. Researchers studied

the genomes of nearly 700,000 people in the US and UK and identified 351 areas in the genome that contribute to whether someone is an early riser. But people who are genetically most likely to be early risers only wake on average 25 minutes earlier than those who aren't, so there are clearly a lot of other factors at play too.

A 2019 study found that one in 300 people has what's called Advanced Sleep Phase, waking naturally well before dawn (between 3:00 a.m. and 5:00 a.m.). The researchers found for roughly one in 500 people, this super early rising runs in the family. These numbers are higher than we previously thought and also suggest a genetic role.

THE BENEFITS OF BEING AN EARLY BIRD

Although we now understand being a night owl is nothing about laziness, there are definitely some costs that come with staying up late. One of the main problems is now known as social jet lag. Normal jet lag is the result of flying to a different time zone and experiencing a mismatch between the time your body thinks it is and the actual time in your new location. Social jet lag is the mismatch between many peoples' body clocks and the waking hours they are forced to keep because of school or work. If your preferred sleep time is 2:00 a.m. to 10:00 a.m., having to be up at 7:00 a.m. for work isn't going to do you any favors.

But there are other problems associated with being a night owl. Night owls consume more caffeine, nicotine, and alcohol. A large twin study found night owls were much more likely to be current and lifelong smokers. Morning people also tend to have better mental health. Night owls are at greater risk of suffering from both depression and schizophrenia. A big international review of studies found evidence that night owls may also be at higher risk of heart disease and type 2 diabetes. The study found those who stay up later at night tended to have more erratic eating habits (for example, missing breakfast) and ate more unhealthy food.

By increasing our exposure to sunlight and reducing our exposure to electrical lighting at night, we can turn our internal clock and sleep times back, and likely make it easier to awaken and be alert in the morning.

Kenneth Wright, Professor of Integrative Physiology, University of Colorado

Research suggests there are also personality differences between morning and night people. Morning people tend to be more proactive, persistent, and cooperative, whereas night owls tend to be more creative and better at risk-taking.

CAN YOU MAKE THE SWITCH?

If you're a night owl who'd like to get up earlier, you probably can if you're willing to change your habits. A recent study of young people whose average preferred sleep time was 3:00 a.m. to 10.30 a.m. showed it's possible to substantially shift sleep times in the space of only one month.

Study volunteers were asked to follow a series of rules: get up two to three hours earlier, have breakfast as soon as they woke up, avoid caffeine after 3:00 p.m., maximize the amount of time they spent outdoors in light during the morning, and not sleep in on weekends. Amazingly, all the participants stuck to the program. Quite possibly because they began to feel much better: less sleepy, stressed, anxious, and depressed. Instead of feeling best in the evening, they now hit their peak in the mid-afternoon.

Other research has shown that when you take people camping and deny them access to all artificial light other than a campfire, their body clocks quickly change. Within a week, former night owls feel sleepy much earlier in the evening and wake with dawn. So if you're a night owl who is keen to make the shift, grab a tent and head for nature. But leave your phone at home.

Why can't I stop drinking coffee?

We've known for a long time that caffeine is a very effective stimulant; it can wake you up, keep you alert, and help you concentrate. Of course, we also know coffee is addictive and it's not surprising we consider addictions to be bad for us. Caffeine is the world's most popular drug. But coffee is more than just caffeine. It's actually chock-a-block full of different compounds, some of them with important health benefits. Some act as antioxidants, others reduce inflammation, and still others regulate insulin (the hormone involved in diabetes).

ARE YOU SURE COFFEE ISN'T BAD FOR ME?

Research published in 2008 found no link between drinking coffee and an increased risk of dying. This study followed about 130,000 people in their 40s and 50s for around 20 years. These volunteers were part of the Nurses' Health Study (all female) and Health Professionals Follow-up Study (all male).

The researchers collected detailed health information about the volunteers, including their diet and coffee-drinking habits. At the same time, they kept records of who died during the study. Even people drinking six cups of coffee a day were not at higher risk of dying.

There's no strong evidence that drinking a few cups of coffee a day is bad for health. If anything, it's the opposite.

Marc Gunter, Doctor of Cancer Epidemiology, Imperial College London

And it gets even better. Not only will coffee not kill you, it may even protect you from a whole heap of nasty illnesses. For example, research indicates coffee consumption reduces the risk of lethal prostate cancer in men. Drinking one to three cups of coffee a day (either normal or decaf), was linked to a 30 percent decreased risk of this cancer. Coffee also appears to reduce the risk of liver cancer by up to 40 percent. Research published in 2017 found coffee is associated with a decreased risk of a number of other kinds of cancer, including breast and colon cancer.

Coffee drinking also reduces the risk of type 2 diabetes. Not only that, but (within limits) the more coffee you drink, the lower your risk. Three to four cups of coffee a day was associated with a 25 percent reduced risk of developing type 2 diabetes, compared with people who drank fewer cups each day. Another study found each additional cup of coffee reduced the risk by a further seven to eight percent. And in type 2 diabetes sufferers, drinking coffee reduced the risk of dying during a 20-year period by 30 percent.

WHAT ABOUT FOR MY BRAIN?

A study published in 2012 followed 124 people aged 65–88 years. All of them were showing the first signs of forgetfulness that can lead to Alzheimer's disease. The researchers measured levels of caffeine in the blood and assessed their brain function over two to four years. Not only was coffee drinking not associated with decreased brain function, people with not much or no caffeine in their bloodstream were much more likely to have progressed to Alzheimer's than people who had three cups' worth of caffeine in their system. Similarly, coffee drinking improves our long-term memory. Researchers found caffeine significantly reduced rates of forgetting over the course of a day. And moderate caffeine intake reduces your risk of getting Parkinson's disease by somewhere between 30 and 60 percent.

WHY THE BAD RAP?

Despite all of this, coffee has a bad name. The negative press is probably because of other behaviors that go hand-in-hand with coffee drinking. People who drink a lot of coffee often smoke, may not exercise very much, and tend to have an unhealthier diet in general. As a result, a lot of early studies that concluded coffee was bad may have been reporting on confounded results. This means it was the smoking, lack of exercise, or diet to blame for poor health, not the coffee drinking.

Too much coffee may still not be a good idea. According to Dr. Rob van Dam: "If you are drinking so much coffee that you get tremors, have sleeping problems, or feel stressed and uncomfortable, then obviously you're drinking too much coffee."

And we know coffee doesn't fully make up for the effects of a lack of sleep. If you rely on coffee as your go-to for getting through each day and concentrating at work, there is some bad news. If you're used to drinking coffee daily, your body will have become tolerant to the effects of the caffeine. So unless you keep upping the number of coffees you're drinking, sadly coffee isn't going to turn you into a ninja at work.

Why do I work better when

If you've ever felt completely engrossed in a task to the point that nothing could distract you, you've experienced what psychologists call "flow," a term coined by Hungarian psychologist Mihály Csíkszentmihályi in 1990. When you're in a state of flow, you're completely focused on whatever you're doing in the present moment. And you're probably performing at your best.

You are most likely to get into the zone when doing your favorite things. Perhaps you've experienced this sensation when running, writing, gaming, playing chess, painting, or playing music. The key factor in flow appears to be the relationship between how difficult a task is and how good you are at it. If it is too challenging you are more likely to end up anxious, scared, or frustrated than in a state of flow.

If, on the other hand, the task is too easy, you'll likely be bored rather than engrossed. You need to find the sweet spot between boredom and stress.

WHEN YOU'RE IN THE ZONE

When you're in a state of flow, your brain is more focused on the subconscious than on conscious thought. The phrase "going with the flow" turns out to be more accurate than we initially assumed: when you're in the zone, the areas of your brain typically involved in decision making are shut off. You don't need high-power thinking or reasoning to solve problems; in flow you know what to do next without thinking about it. Things simply flow!

Shutting off some of your higher-power thinking (located in your brain's prefrontal cortex) has other fascinating consequences. With this part of the brain less active, you are less likely to

I'm in the zone?

self-monitor. You end up less critical, more creative, and more courageous. When scientists scanned the brains of improvising jazz piano players they found the musicians' brains were much less active than normal in the areas responsible for planning and self-censoring. This results in the players feeling less inhibited, with the parts of the brain involved with self-expression far more active.

Your brainwaves also change when you're in flow. Instead of the usual fast-moving waves when you're awake, your brainwaves slow down to daydreaming speed which fosters creativity. At the same time, your brain is flooded with feel-good chemicals which increase your focus and ability to link ideas in new ways.

THE DARK ZONE

But there's a dark side to this state of flow. Christened the "machine zone,"

it's when you completely zone out. Perhaps it happens when you're scrolling through your social media feed, aka doom scrolling. You get into a rhythm—scroll, click like, scroll more, and repeat. Everything else fades away, time disappears, and you are fully immersed in...Instagram.

As anyone who has ever been sucked into playing a poker machine knows, this zone can be tough to leave. You're in the zone, but without the pleasure, mastery, or meaning. So next time you find yourself in the machine zone, walk away. Instead, lose yourself in doing something you love.

Why do I stick my tongue out when I'm concentrating?

Next time you have the opportunity, watch a young child who is concentrating hard on doing something with their hands. Chances are, you'll notice their tongue poking out from their mouth. Is it simply a childhood idiosyncrasy, or could there be more to the humble poking tongue?

Think back to the last time you did something with your hands that required a lot of dexterity, like threading a needle or sinking the perfect shot while playing pool. It's highly likely your tongue was pressed between your lips, perhaps with the tip peeking out. Your tongue is one of the largest groups of muscles in your body and there's good reason to think our tendency to poke it out when concentrating is more than just a quirk.

DON'T INTERRUPT ME!

Research published back in 1974 looked at "tongue-show behavior" in young children, young gorillas, and adults living in a variety of countries. The researchers concluded that humans (and other primates) show our tongues to communicate when we don't want to interact with anyone. During the 1980s, a number of researchers explored the idea a tongue poking out effectively signals: "Don't disturb me." In one study, 50 university students each took an individual reading comprehension test. The lecturer

sat at the front of the room wearing headphones. Each student was put in the position in which they had to interrupt the lecturer: one page of the test was clearly missing. Because of the headphones, a student had to either call loudly or tap the lecturer on the arm to get attention. If the lecturer appeared to be concentrating and had their tongue poking out, it took students on average nearly 20 seconds to interrupt and ask for the extra page. If the lecturer at the front had the same facial expression—but without a visible tongue—students waited an average of only seven seconds before interrupting. People are much less likely to interrupt you if your tongue is poking out than if you simply look to be concentrating intensely.

> *This isn't just a cute quirk of childhood... rather the behavior fits the theory that spoken language originally evolved from gestures.*
>
> Dr. Christian Jarrett, psychologist and author

IT'S ALL ABOUT LANGUAGE

Tongues have a big supply of nerves, making them incredibly sensitive. It isn't just responsible for tasting things but provides you with a detailed and constantly updated mental map of the inside of your mouth. You may also find that as you think, your tongue moves to partly form the shape of a word you are thinking. Your tongue is sending lots of information to your brain all the time. So perhaps in order to reduce some of this sensory input, you stick your tongue outside of your mouth and hold it still. As a result, you are left with more brainpower to concentrate on a demanding task.

We know there are strong links between the brain regions responsible for speaking and the control of our hands and arms. And many scientists have suggested human speech may have evolved from communication by hand gestures. In a recent study, right-handed four-year-olds were filmed while completing tasks requiring either very fine hand control (opening a padlock with a key), less fine control (playing a game that involved knocking or tapping the table), or no hand control at all (remembering a story). The researchers watched each video for any sign of tongues poking out.

All of the children stuck their tongues out while performing the tasks, but more often during some tasks than others. Although we might expect something as challenging as opening the padlock to lead to the most tongue-showing, that's not what the researchers found. It was the knock and tap game that resulted in the kids sticking out their tongues most often.

This is explained by the fact the game involved strict rules, rapid turn-taking, and the use of defined hand gestures—all of which are basic and early components of language. To back this up, the researchers noticed that the tongue most often poked out on the right side of the body. That suggests the tongue movement is being controlled by the left side of the brain, which is where language centers are usually found in right-handed people (particularly among children).

If kids can't help but stick their tongues out when engaging the language centers of their brains, why don't more adults do the same? Probably because adults have trained themselves not to do it out of embarrassment.

So next time you see someone's tongue sticking out as they concentrate, smile by all means and take it as a sign to leave them in peace. But also step back and admire a sign that the complex language we all depend on may well have evolved from simple hand gestures.

Why do I panic when I'm i

Around five percent of the world's population is thought to experience claustrophobia, and women are more likely to suffer than men. The severity of symptoms vary: in extreme cases a person may choose to walk dozens of flights of stairs rather than take the elevator or refuse to get on an underground train for decades.

GET OUTTA MY SPACE

Why do only some people experience claustrophobia when few of us like feeling trapped?

There are a few different theories as to what causes it. In many cases, claustrophobia is the result of a traumatic experience like being stuck in an elevator. It's hardly surprising that after being trapped somewhere we feel anxious about going back into that place. But research suggests some people are also predisposed to feeling claustrophobic. A number

of researchers have looked at the relationship between anxiety disorders and the size of the amygdala—the almond-shaped groups of nerve cells deep in your brain involved with processing emotions like fear. The research findings have been mixed but some studies found people with panic disorders have smaller amygdalae than average. Perhaps someone with smaller amygdalae perceives the risk of danger differently and these are the people more likely to experience claustrophobia.

A few years ago, other researchers found that a mistake in a single gene causes claustrophobia-like symptoms in mice. Humans have the same gene, found in an area of a chromosome linked to panic disorders. If a defect in this gene can also explain claustrophobia in people, the fact is some of us simply have claustrophobia in our genes.

the elevator?

Another study connected people's perception of their personal space to claustrophobia. We all have a perception of how far our personal space extends beyond our body—interestingly this distance is related to arm length. This personal space is our comfort zone, and we are very aware of anything entering it. People who experience claustrophobia tend to feel their personal space extends farther than we would normally predict. For these people, there are more frequent intrusions into that personal space; they are more likely to feel like someone or something is "in their face."

CLAUSTROPHOBIA MAKES SENSE

There are several treatments for claustrophobia. Virtual reality has been used to reduce fear of confined spaces and cognitive behavioral therapy also helps many claustrophobes. Some claustrophobes find that being forced to face their fears helps. Although terrifying at the time, people find their panic eventually disappears.

While claustrophobia sufferers may be desperate to find a cure for their fears, it's worth considering why we experience claustrophobia. From an evolutionary point of view, claustrophobia makes sense. Of course we've evolved to be fearful of being trapped in a confined space; many of the situations that result in us feeling trapped are life-threatening. Whether a collapsed cave or building, we have every reason to fear for our lives. It's to be expected that we've evolved to hate the feeling of being confined. The problem comes when a non-life-threatening situation evokes the same paralyzing fear.

IT'S FRIDAY AFTERNOON. YOU'VE KNOWN FOR WEEKS YOUR FINAL REPORT IS DUE
BY THE END OF THE DAY BUT SOMEHOW YOU'VE MANAGED TO
PUT OFF WORKING ON IT UNTIL NOW. SOUND FAMILIAR?

Why do I keep putting things off?

Procrastination is "voluntarily delaying an intended course of action despite expecting to be worse off for the delay." It's tempting to imagine procrastination is a recent thing, a result of the constant barrage of social media and other digital distractions we all experience. But procrastination has been around for centuries.

Egyptologist Ronald Leprohon translated some hieroglyphics from 1400 BCE as "Friend, stop putting off work and allow us to go home in good time." And the Greek poet Hesiod advised not to "put your work off till tomorrow and the day after" back in 800 BCE. Ancient Greek philosophers coined the term *Akrasia*, which is a state of acting against your better judgment.

In a study of more than 1,300 adults from six countries, about a quarter of people reported that procrastination was one of their defining personality traits. Other research found one in five people qualify as a chronic procrastinator. In a study of university students, only one percent reported they never procrastinate.

THE PROCRASTINATION WAR
One of the first studies attempting to get a handle on the effects of

procrastination followed the academic performance, stress, general health, and procrastination habits of US college students in 1997. In the short-term, procrastinators were less stressed than others, presumably because they chose fun over study. But in the long run, procrastinators got lower marks and experienced greater stress and more illness compared with non-procrastinators. Since then, the evidence has been mounting: putting things off can seriously undermine your well-being.

Maybe it's boring, or frustrating, or maybe it scares the heck out of you and you feel like an imposter or failure.

Tim Pychyl, Associate Professor of Psychology, Carleton University

Procrastination has been the subject of much research over recent decades, and there's no one cause. Despite the fact procrastination is commonly associated with laziness, it has very little to do with time management skills. Put simply, procrastination is a war between two parts of our brain: the limbic system (think of it as your inner four-year-old) and the prefrontal cortex. The limbic system seeks instant gratification while the prefrontal cortex is involved with planning and decision making.

The limbic system is one of the oldest parts of our brains and tends to function on autopilot. Anytime you're not consciously engaged with a task, the limbic system leads you to give in to what feels immediately good. As a result, we value immediate rewards much more highly than future ones.

In contrast, it takes effort to kick the more recently evolved prefrontal cortex into action. This means that distant rewards, even if they are big ones, don't have much sway over us compared with immediate pleasure.

Procrastination isn't just a bad habit; it's pretty much hardwired into your brain. Recent research suggests procrastination may have

more to do with managing emotions than time. Brain scans suggest people who procrastinate more are less successful at filtering out emotions and distractions. Piers Steel from the University of Calgary is one of the world's experts on procrastination. He analyzed more than 200 procrastination studies and found a clear link between impulsiveness and procrastination. People who tend to act impulsively are also likely to procrastinate a lot. In the case of acting impulsively, we should wait but instead do whatever it is right now. In the case of procrastinating, we should do something right now but instead we wait. The common feature is self-control.

ASK YOURSELF WHY

What can you do next time you find yourself procrastinating? Perhaps the most important thing is to notice you're procrastinating and ask yourself why. Is the task too big and overwhelming? Are you lacking some of the tools you need to get it done? Are you surrounded by too many distractions? Are you lacking confidence? Perhaps you are putting off the task because you don't think you'll be able to do it well.

Interestingly, one study found forgiving yourself for procrastinating makes it less likely you will procrastinate next time. By forgiving ourselves, we minimize the negative feelings we associate with a task that can lead us to avoid doing it again. And if you can focus on how good you'll feel once something is done, you'll have much more motivation in the here and now to get started on it.

So, instead of reading this, is there something else you should be doing right now?

HOW MANY DIFFERENT THINGS ARE YOU TRYING TO DO RIGHT NOW? IT'S EASY TO THINK YOU'LL BE MORE PRODUCTIVE BY DOING LOTS OF THINGS AT ONCE. BUT EFFECTIVE MULTITASKING IS AN ILLUSION.

Why can't I multitask?

With the exception of texting while driving, many of us think multitasking is something to aspire to. But the reality is, trying to do multiple things at once actually slows us down and leads to more mistakes. We are simply no good at trying to engage with more than one decision-making process at a time.

In fact, experts tell us even the term multitasking is wrong: we should call it task switching. Researchers suggest we may lose up to 40 percent of our productivity by trying to multitask. What feels like multitasking is actually rapid switching between tasks and the time it takes to switch between tasks all adds up.

Think it only takes a few seconds to jump between reading emails and the report you urgently need to write? No big deal unless you are switching every time you get a new email notification. And how long does it take you to get to the point where you are writing effectively again? Research shows it takes an average of 23 minutes. In some cases, study volunteers never got back into the flow of writing.

SOME TASKS ARE EASIER THAN OTHERS
If multitasking is so hard, perhaps you're wondering why you can read this book, eat your lunch, and listen to music all at once. How easy it is to

juggle tasks depends on how engaged your prefrontal cortex is during the activity. Natural behaviors like walking, talking, and eating don't take a lot of brain effort so we can do those things at the same time as paying attention to something else. Having said that, talking on your phone while driving increases your risk of having an accident four-fold. It's been shown to be equivalent to driving with a blood alcohol reading of about 0.08 (the legal threshold for intoxication).

In one study, when 56,000 people were observed approaching an intersection in their cars, those who were talking on their cell phones were ten times less likely to actually stop at the stop sign. Even walking at the same time as talking on your cell phone takes up most of your brain's attention. Only one quarter of people doing both noticed a clown on a unicycle ride past them who had been planted there by researchers.

As soon as there are multiple tasks which require thinking, it becomes clear our brains simply aren't wired for multitasking.

THERE ARE SUPERTASKERS AMONG US

But all is not lost. Research has uncovered a small proportion of the population—about two percent—who have extraordinary multitasking abilities. Imagine simultaneously doing a driving test, solving complex math problems, and doing memory tests on your phone. People who can easily do that have been called supertaskers and they have brains that actually become less active the more tasks they are trying to do at once. And that's not all. Supertaskers do better, not worse, at each individual task the more simultaneous tasks they are doing.

The irony is that as soon as we hear that supertaskers exist, 90 percent of us decide we belong in that two percent. But research has shown that the people who multitask the most—and are the most confident in their multitasking abilities—tend to be the worst at it.

Multitasking is like constantly pulling up a plant. This kind of constant shifting of your attention means that new ideas and concepts have no chance to take root and flourish.

Barbara Oakley, Professor of Engineering, Oakland University

THE COST OF MULTITASKING

Assuming you are not a supertasker, it's worth considering what our attempts at multitasking cost us. Research suggests the more we attempt to multitask, the more we are training ourselves not to focus. We are effectively teaching ourselves that something unknown—an unread email or the next notification—is always more worthy of our attention than whatever task we are meant to be working on.

We sacrifice focus in order to ensure we don't miss any unexpected surprises, but in the process, we lose our ability to block out distractions. And that means we're not very good at getting stuff done or thinking deeply about things. As Cal Newport says in his book *Deep Work*: "Efforts to deepen your focus will struggle if you don't simultaneously wean your mind from a dependence on distraction."

Why don't I remember why I

Most of us have had the experience of walking into a room and feeling confused. Researchers have used a few different experiments to try and understand what's going on. First, they got people playing a video game. In the game, players used arrow keys to move around a virtual space. Their task was to pick up a colored object from a table, move to another table, put the object down, and pick up another one. Sounds pretty simple. But once they had picked it up, the players could no longer see what they were carrying.

At various times, the researchers asked the players the color and shape of the object they were carrying. It turned out that if the player had just moved through a doorway in the game, they were much worse at remembering—worse than if they had moved the same distance within the same room.

Next, the researchers recreated the game in real life. Volunteers walked around, picking up and putting down objects on real tables, carrying the objects in shoeboxes so they couldn't see them. Sure enough, even when people walked exactly the same distance, their memory of what was in the box was much worse if they had walked through a door. People were two or three times more likely to forget after walking through a doorway.

YOU'VE WALKED INTO A ROOM WITH A CLEAR PURPOSE IN MIND. EXCEPT NOW YOU CAN'T REMEMBER WHAT IT WAS. IS IT JUST YOUR IMAGINATION, OR DOES WALKING INTO A DIFFERENT ROOM MAKE YOU FORGET?

walked into this room?

LOCATION, LOCATION, LOCATION

You might think all these players needed to do was go back to the room they were originally in to remember what they were carrying. Psychologists call this the encoding specificity principle. The idea is you'll remember something better in the same context as you first took in the information. But the researchers tested this too, and found that going back to the original room where they picked up the object didn't help people to remember what they were carrying.

OUT WITH THE OLD, IN WITH THE NEW

Researchers have now christened this the Doorway Effect, and it explains some interesting things about how our memories work: as it's not possible to have all the information stored in your brain constantly at hand, we break up thoughts and memories into separate episodes or events.

Once a particular event is over, our brains discard some of the old information, ready for new, more relevant things. How do we decide when an event is over? Research suggests one of the many triggers for our brains to decide a new event has begun is walking through a doorway, otherwise known as an event boundary.

When you pass through a doorway, it signals to your brain that something new has begun. Information that was relevant in the previous room isn't as relevant or important now. Amazingly, even just imagining walking through a door was enough to make people forget things more easily.

What can we do about the Doorway Effect? Not much, unless you want to follow Professor Gabriel Radvansky's advice: "Doorways are bad. Avoid them at all costs."

YOU SPEND ABOUT 10 PERCENT OF THE TIME YOU'RE AWAKE WITH YOUR EYES CLOSED—BLINKING. BUT WHY DO WE BLINK SO OFTEN AND WHY DON'T WE NOTICE THE WORLD PLUNGE INTO DARKNESS EVERY TIME WE DO?

Why do I blink so much?

If you're awake for 16 hours a day, you have your eyes closed for more than an hour and a half each day. That seems a lot and suggests blinking must be doing something important. The most obvious explanation for blinking is the fact that a blink clears away any pesky dust particles that might have landed on your eye. Blinking also keeps your eyeball moist. Each blink lasts only a fraction of a second, but that's enough time to spread the perfect mix of lubricating fluids across the surface of your eye. Is it as simple as that? Yes, and no.

The act of blinking does keep our eyes clean and lubricated, but research has shown we wouldn't need to blink nearly so often if that were the main game. Think about the last time you had a staring competition: you were easily able to stop blinking for far longer than a few seconds. There's more going on when we blink than just a cleaning service.

A clue to the role of blinking is when we blink. You might think blinking is random, but it's not. We blink at predictable times. When reading, we blink at the end of a sentence. When listening to someone talking, we blink during natural pauses in speaking. And when watching a movie, we blink during scenes when the action lags. Perhaps just after something important has happened or when the main character is briefly out of shot. And what's

more, if we're watching with friends, our blinks tend to be synchronized with theirs. One fascinating study found that skilled magicians take advantage of synchronized blinking to hide the secret of their illusions.

A MOMENT OF CALM

Scientists interested in the timing of our blinks measured people's brain activity while watching *Mr. Bean*. (Apparently the actor Rowan Atkinson is very effective at synchronizing blinks.) The idea was to work out which parts of the brain were more or less active during blinking. They found that during blinking, there's a spike in activity in the areas of our brain involved with the "default mode of brain function." Default mode is how your brain operates when you're in a state of calm, wakeful rest, not distracted by what's going on in the outside world. It's the same mode of brain function often brought on by silence (see page 26). Perhaps blinking is a way to snatch a quick mental time-out every few seconds.

To test if this little mental break is simply the result of not seeing anything for a brief moment, the researchers inserted tiny blackouts in the video—a blank screen that lasted for the same amount of time as a blink. But, looking at the brain again, the default mode didn't kick in during the blackouts. So, for our brains, blinking is more than not seeing for a moment. The researchers suggested these brief moments of calm and introspection may help us to focus and to pay more attention to the world around us when we open our eyes again.

I CAN SEE THE LIGHT

An odd thing about blinking is that we're barely aware we do it. If you were to sit in a windowless room with the lights being turned off and then on again every few seconds, you would certainly notice. In fact, you'd probably become pretty annoyed. But that's similar to what's happening every time you blink: the world goes dark for a moment. Yet we don't feel as though our view of the world around us has been interrupted at all.

What is going on in our brains to allow us to be oblivious to these moments of darkness? Recent research tested two possible answers. Firstly, that after each blink, our brain backdates what we see. In this case, we assume what we see after a blink was also true during the time our eyes were closed. Our brain simply fills in the gap. A second possibility is that our brains hold onto the image of what the world looked like before the blink and assume this to have continued during the time our eyes were closed.

Our brains do a lot of prediction to compensate for how we move around in the world, like a steadicam of the mind.

Patrick Cavanagh, Professor of Psychology, Harvard University

To test these two possibilities, scientists used some experiments involving flashing a letter on a screen. Students taking part in the study had to say how long the letter appeared on the screen when they were allowed to blink, and again when they weren't. But the results of the study suggest neither of these theories is right.

The study participants simply underestimated the time the letter was visible for when they blinked. This suggests our brains just ignore blinks, momentarily shutting down our perceptions of the outside world. What we still don't know is how our brains make the world appear continuous despite our blinks. But next time someone says "Don't blink or you'll miss it," remember that a blink may be just the time-out your brain needs.

Why do I blush?

According to Charles Darwin, "Blushing is the most peculiar and most human of all expressions." He sent letters to colony administrators and missionaries all over the world to find out the answer to one simple question: Do all humans blush? The answer is yes. Blushing is one of the things that sets us apart from all other animals. Unlike most expressions, no equivalent has been found in any animal.

The process of the skin on your face turning crimson isn't complicated. The muscles in the walls of your veins relax and allow more blood to flow. Blood flow to your skin is controlled by the sympathetic nervous system (the part of your nervous system responsible for the fight or flight response). When this part of your nervous system is activated, the hormone adrenaline is released into your system. Adrenaline acts as a stimulant. Your blood vessels dilate to improve blood flow and maximize the delivery of oxygen to your muscles. You're ready to put up a good fight or get the hell out.

I'M SO EMBARRASSED

But sometimes, the veins in your face also respond to the adrenaline: they dilate and let more blood flow through them than usual. This increased blood flow is responsible for the spreading crimson and warmth we call

blushing. As you may have experienced first-hand, we have no control over it. You can't blush on command and neither can you stop blushing when you want to. The interesting thing is that in other parts of your body, your veins don't do much in the presence of adrenaline.

So why do our cheeks go bright red? We don't know for sure, but we do know there are specific triggers for blushing: we blush when we're feeling embarrassed, ashamed, or exposed. Blushing occurs when we are receiving unwanted social attention. It seems cruel that at the exact moment we wish the floor would swallow us up because we're so embarrassed, our cheeks turn flame-red, drawing even more attention to ourselves. Even being told we are blushing when we're not can cause many of us to visibly blush.

> *A blush is involuntary and uncontrollable— an actor might simulate a smile, laughter, or a frown, but not a blush.*
>
> Ray Crozier, Professor of Psychology, Cardiff University

WHEN BLUSHING IS A PROBLEM

Chronic blushing—when a person blushes more often and more obviously than most of us—is also a debilitating condition. About five percent of the population suffer from it and a quick read of an online support page reveals stories of sufferers feeling unable to leave the house. Chronic blushers blush in normal social situations that wouldn't usually result in blushing, for example, in response to someone saying their name. There are a few different treatment options for chronic blushers: some sufferers use corrective makeup, others have success with medication, others find relief with cognitive behavioral therapy or hypnotherapy.

A more controversial response is surgery: cutting the nerves responsible for blushing. These are the nerves that cause the veins in the face to dilate and are usually cut under the armpit. This surgery has mixed reviews: while many patients report it solves their blushing problem, some are unhappy. Because the nerves involved with blushing are also involved in sweating, some patients end up with a different, but equally unsettling problem. Post-surgery, patients are unable to sweat from the face, which can lead to excessive sweating in other parts of the body.

THE BENEFITS OF BLUSHING

All of this begs the question: Why have we evolved to blush? Can there be any benefit to that hot glow of embarrassment most of us have experienced? Research suggests the answer is a definite yes. One study demonstrated we are more likely to trust people who are easily embarrassed. For example, we are far more likely to trust and want to befriend someone who shows embarrassment rather than pride at being told they've done well on a test.

And what of blushing itself? A number of studies point to the fact blushing may have evolved as a way of signaling regret or remorse. Blushing signals we know we've done the wrong thing and we're sorry. Blushing is reliable evidence of the fact we genuinely feel bad about having done something wrong because it can't be faked. Because it's out of your control, blushing is much more reliable than a verbal "sorry." We trust and forgive people who blush more than those who don't: a number of researchers believe blushing is an important part of the social glue that keeps human societies functioning. So next time you feel that familiar warm glow of discomfort, try to remember there is an upside. You're telling the world you can be trusted.

Why is holding eye contact so exhausting?

From birth, we prefer looking at faces that look directly at us (see page 44). And from a very early age, our brains respond more to a face looking into our eyes than one looking away. We've evolved to have eyes that make it extremely obvious which direction we are looking: no other primate has an exposed white area around the colored iris as we do.

When someone makes frequent eye contact with us, we tend to judge that person—at least in Western cultures— as more likable, trustworthy, intelligent, and having higher self-esteem than someone who makes less eye contact. We also rate a stranger we've made eye contact with as more similar to us in their personality and appearance than another stranger.

LOOK AT ME

Making eye contact with someone makes us feel good. But you've probably also experienced the sensation of discomfort and vulnerability that comes with holding eye contact for too long. How long is too long?

Researchers asked 500 volunteers to watch a video in which an actor looked directly at them for somewhere between one-tenth of a second and ten seconds. The volunteers pressed a button as soon as they felt the actor had looked at them for an uncomfortably long period. The average preferred length of eye contact was 3.3 seconds (too quick a glance and the study participants felt the actor was sneaky or suspicious).

What happens if you maintain eye contact with someone beyond what feels comfortable? People who sat in pairs, looking into each other's eyes for ten minutes reported entering an altered state of consciousness. Half of them said they'd seen their own face in their partner's face, 75 percent reported having seen a monster, and 90 percent of the study participants said their partner's face had looked deformed. Perhaps there's a good reason why we feel the urge to look away!

LOOK AWAY

Have you ever noticed someone repeatedly breaking off eye contact with you during a conversation? Or perhaps you've found yourself needing to look away to think when someone asks you a difficult question?

In 1988, researchers showed the more our brains are working on a particular task, the more likely we are to look away from someone's gaze. It isn't because of embarrassment or shyness; looking away allowed people to perform better on memory and general knowledge tests. Recently, researchers in Japan tested the effect further by asking volunteers to play word association games while looking at a computer-generated face. At different times, the volunteers were asked to either maintain eye contact, or look away. The researchers found it was harder for people to come up with appropriate words when making eye contact. And the less familiar the word a participant in the study was searching for, the harder it became for that person to keep their attention on the face.

It seems maintaining eye contact is so mentally stimulating, our brains become overloaded when trying to think and hold someone's gaze at the same time. If thinking clearly is the priority, we look away. So next time you're talking with someone and they look away, don't assume it means they're bored. Just the opposite: it may well be a sign that your conversation is so interesting their brain is working overtime.

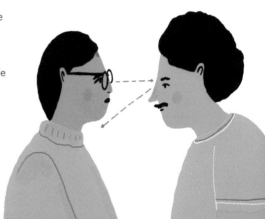

Why can't I get that song out of my head?

The term *ohrwurm* was coined in 1979 by psychiatrist Cornelius Eckert.
Other names include tune wedgies, sticky tunes, and stuck song syndrome.
The Italians call them *canzone tormentone*—tormenting songs. *Ohrwürmer*
(earworms) aren't necessarily good or bad songs, but they are catchy and
tend to be extremely annoying because they are hard to get rid of. Research
has found 91 percent of people have an earworm once a week, and a
quarter of people have one once a day. Fifteen percent of people say they
find earworms disturbing.

Interestingly, music pops into our heads unexpectedly and involuntarily
much more often than visual images, words, or smells. The likelihood of
getting an earworm seems to come down to three things: the music, the
person, and the situation.

WHAT MAKES A GOOD WURM?
Researchers at the University of London have found that under the right
circumstances, most songs can become earworms. But it is much more
common for a song we know to get stuck, and songs with lyrics lodge
in our minds much more often than instrumental pieces. Earworms last
between about eight and 15 seconds and tend to follow a musical magic

formula. The key components are musical notes with longer durations but short intervals between the notes (such as playing keys that sit close to one another on a piano). That's not surprising given those features also make songs easier to sing.

Earworms tend to be predictable and repetitive, but with enough variety to keep you interested. Classic earworm songs are Starship's "We Built this City," ABBA's "Waterloo," the Baha Men's "Who Let the Dogs Out?," and Taylor Swift's "Shake it Off."

WHY ME? WHY NOW?

Musicians experience more earworms than non-musicians because the act of practicing or performing music makes you more susceptible to getting a tune lodged in your head.

People who believe music is important (even if they haven't had any musical training) are also more likely to get songs stuck in their head than people who don't care as much for music. If you tend to sing or dance along to songs, you may also be more likely to catch an earworm.

Unsurprisingly, if you have recently listened to a particular song, it is more likely to stick in your mind. Similarly, if you have heard a song repeatedly, the chances are higher it will become an earworm. And of course, if it is a song that is easy to sing, the act of singing it yourself makes it more likely the song will stick around even after you've had enough.

Memories can also have a lot to do with it. For example, being in a particular place may trigger an associated song to come into your mind.

If earworms are something that plague you often, it's worth knowing we are all more likely to get stuck with an earworm when we are tired, stressed, or bored: research has found waiting in line is a common time to develop an earworm.

...this little fragment, often a bit of the chorus of the song, that just plays and replays like it's stuck on loop in your head.

Jennifer Talarico, Professor of Psychology, Lafayette College

HOW DO YOU DISLODGE A WURM?

There are two ways you can respond to having an earworm: you can try to distract yourself, or you can simply cope—which probably means putting up with it until the worm disappears of its own accord. Distraction might involve tackling a crossword or sudoku puzzle, starting a conversation, or listening to different music. One study suggested that chewing gum may be a solution to unwanted earworms. People who chewed gum straight after hearing a catchy tune were 30 percent less likely to end up with an earworm. The theory is that when we have an earworm, we are saying the words of the song in our heads and chewing interrupts this process.

Other recent research found that for many people, there is a clear winner when it comes to strategies to get rid of an earworm—but it's not going to be fun if the earworm happens to be a song you hate. You have to tackle your earworm headfirst and listen to it intentionally. Better yet: sing it out loud. Wurm, be gone.

Why do I see faces in

You've probably heard about Jesus on a banana peel, the Man in the Moon, and the face of Madonna on a toasted sandwich (which sold for $28,000). We've seen peppers that look like British politicians and a crab tainted with the face of Osama bin Laden.

Since the 1700s, the surface of Mars has been a particularly rich source of these illusions. In 1976, people were captivated by images of a face on Mars, which turned out to be nothing more than a trick of light and shadows. Mars also boasts a smiley face in a crater, a lava flow that resembles Kermit the Frog, the face of Mahatma Gandhi, a rat, and Bigfoot. Famous cases aside, people have spied faces in plug sockets, trees, buildings, rocks, and USB drives.

FACES, FACES EVERYWHERE
There are many different kinds of pareidolia, but seeing faces is the most common. Why are we so quick to see a face where there isn't one? Simple— because we spend so much of our time looking at faces. And we've evolved to depend on our ability to recognize and extract information from these faces.

We are hardwired to recognize faces: our social lives have long relied on us being able to spot a face from a distance or in low light. Not only that, but it's extremely useful to be able to deduce other things from a face: mood, age, gender, and the direction a person is looking. Is this person a friend, or a threat? Even as very young babies, we prefer to look at faces over non-faces (see page 96).

everyday

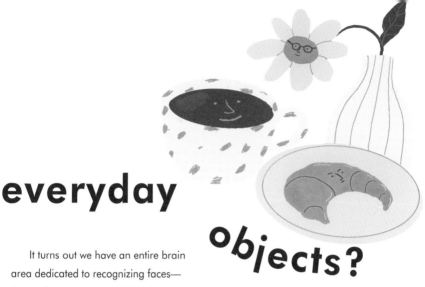

objects?

It turns out we have an entire brain area dedicated to recognizing faces—the Fusiform Face Area (FFA). This area is active when we see a face, even in blind people (see page 44). Research shows this area of the brain lights up in the same way when we see an illusory face as when we see a real face. The FFA is active when a person reports seeing a face, even when there is absolutely no pattern (in a pure noise image).

TRUE BELIEVERS

Identifying patterns is nothing new—it's the basis of the infamous Rorschach inkblot test. But some of us are more likely to see faces than others. A Finnish study firstly asked volunteers whether they saw faces in dozens of objects and landscapes. The researchers then asked about the belief systems of the participants. Did each person believe in

God? And how about the paranormal? Religious people and those who believed in the paranormal were much more likely to see faces than atheists and skeptics. "Believers" were also more likely to see emotions in the illusory faces.

And if you're thinking our ability to see faces in toast, tortillas, and toilets is something that makes us uniquely human, think again. Recent research shows rhesus monkeys see faces that aren't there too. And it makes perfect sense—if a monkey thinks it sees a tiger when there's no tiger around, it isn't a big deal. But the consequences of not spotting a real tiger might not be so pretty. It's not just humans who have evolved to be highly tuned to faces.

Why do I take so many photos?

Every day around the world we take billions of photos. Gone are the days of carefully choosing which images to preserve on our precious 24- or 36-roll film. We can capture as many moments as we like, safely preserved digitally to help us remember people and places. But does taking a photo of an event change how we remember it? The answer is yes.

In one study, students were led on a guided tour of the Bellarmine Museum of Art. They were asked to take photos of some artworks and simply observe others. The next day, researchers asked questions to find out how much the students remembered about different artworks. Not only did the students remember fewer of the artworks they had photographed, they also didn't remember as many of the specific details about the art.

In another study, a few hundred people went on a self-guided tour of the Stanford University Memorial Church. Some of them were instructed to take photos of the building's features, some went in empty-handed. A week later, they were all given a surprise quiz, designed to check how much they remembered about the building. The results were the same: those who had taken photos remembered significantly less than the people who simply looked around. This phenomenon has been dubbed the photo-taking-impairment effect.

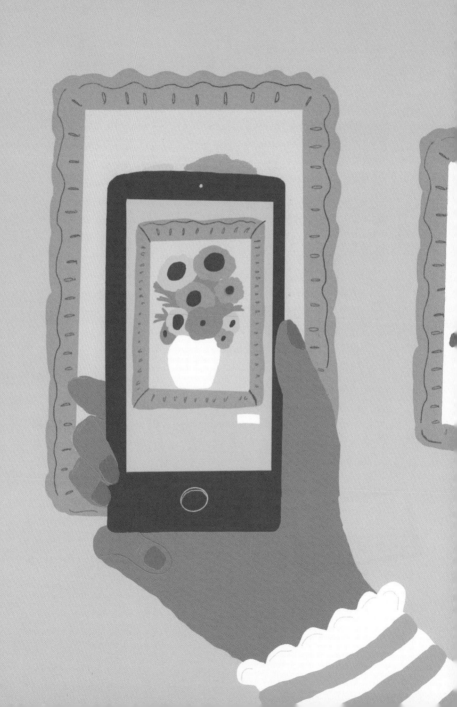

OUTSOURCING REMEMBERING

One explanation of this effect is cognitive offloading. We are outsourcing the act of remembering things to our photos. A well-known study published in 2011 showed that if people are told a computer will save a piece of information, they are less likely to remember it themselves. The idea is that if we know we can rely on our photos rather than our brains, there's no need for us to mentally store the information for later.

But researchers have also explored the role of cognitive offloading in photography more directly. In one experiment, people knowingly took photos for Snapchat (an app where photos and videos disappear soon after sharing). In another experiment, some of the study volunteers knew they would be asked to manually delete the photos after taking them. Despite knowing they wouldn't have ongoing access to the photos, these people experienced the photo-taking-impairment effect just as strongly as those who believed they would get to keep the photos.

This leads us to think there's more than cognitive offloading going on. Perhaps a big part of the problem is quite simple: when our attention is focused on taking photos, we're distracted from what's around us.

WHO ARE YOU TAKING PHOTOS FOR?

Interestingly, researchers have shown our reasons for taking a photo of an experience changes how much we enjoy the experience. If we take photos simply for ourselves—to remember an experience—the act of taking photos doesn't interfere with our enjoyment. But if we take photos with the intention of sharing them with other people, we don't enjoy ourselves as much. Why? Probably because we become self-conscious about how we're presenting ourselves. Our attention is focused on how the photo looks, rather than on the experience itself.

Interestingly, whether we take selfies or photos without ourselves in them also affects our memory of the experience itself.

Research shows that if you're in the photo, your perspective changes—you feel more emotionally removed from the original event. It's as though you're looking at it through someone else's eyes rather than experiencing it yourself. And if our memories of an event are influenced by our selfies taken at the event, it means we're remembering the event based on how we wanted to portray it to other people, rather than what it actually felt like to be there.

TO SNAP OR NOT TO SNAP

So what are we to do? Stop taking photos altogether? Or at least stop posting them on social media? Stop taking selfies? Not necessarily, but we should probably think about how often we take photos as opposed to just being in the moment.

We could also think about the kinds of photos we take. In the art museum study, people who zoomed in and took close-up photos of the art remembered much more than people who just snapped a photo of the whole work. Presumably it took time and thought to choose the right angle for the close-up. Quite different to standing square in front of an artwork, photographing the whole thing and walking away.

Research has also shown that if we take a photo of something, our memory is biased toward what we could see, as opposed to what we could hear or smell. Perhaps the best plan is to snap a quick photo with no intention to share it, then put away our phones. Then we can look, listen, and sniff at what's around us, and really remember the moment.

> *People so often whip out their cameras almost mindlessly to capture a moment, to the point that they are missing what is happening right in front of them.*

Linda Henkel, Professor of Psychology, Fairfield University

Why do I like doodling?

As adults, we often draw during meetings, on the margins of the agenda papers. We try to hide the fact we're drawing because we're worried about the impression it creates. We think someone who's doodling is not doing what they are supposed to be doing: that is, listening. Even the word doodle carries negative connotations. In the eighteenth century, to "doodle" meant to swindle or ridicule someone. A century later, a "doodle" was a corrupt politician.

DOODLING IS A LONG WAY FROM BEING A BAD HABIT

We now know just how wrong many assumptions about doodling are: doodling isn't a waste of time. Doodling is a powerful way to improve listening,

thinking, focus, and concentration. We rarely set out to doodle; doodling is just what happens when our brains are processing information.

One of the first studies that aimed to test whether doodling improves concentration asked people to listen to a monotonous telephone message. Their job was to listen for the names of people coming to a party among lots of irrelevant information. Half of the listeners were asked to doodle, the rest had to listen without anything else to do. When they were given a surprise memory test, the doodlers remembered a third more names than those who had concentrated only on the message. The researchers believe doodling prevented the listeners from daydreaming and getting distracted.

DRAWING TO REMEMBER

Forget surprise memory tests: if you know you need to remember something, try drawing it. In one study, 14-year-olds were given 850 words to read about the biology of flu. It was hard to read, and the students knew they were going to be tested on what they had learned. Half the students were asked to make a drawing to represent each of the seven paragraphs, the rest simply read the text. When they were later tested on how much of the science they had understood and remembered, the drawers did way better. In a second experiment, the same was true even when the reading-only group was given the text with drawings already provided. It was the act of drawing their own pictures that resulted in those students remembering what they had read.

In another series of experiments, researchers tested whether it was easier to memorize a series of words by writing or drawing. University students were given a list of easily-drawn words like "apple." For each word, the students had 40 seconds to either draw the object, or write the word repeatedly. Later the students were given a minute to remember as many of the words as they could. The drawing students remembered twice as many words as the writing ones. Again, looking at pictures drawn by someone else didn't have the same effect. Even when the students were only given four seconds for their drawings, these students had a huge advantage in later memory: the quality of the drawing didn't matter.

So it doesn't matter whether we think we're any good at it or not. The time has come for us all to get doodling.

HOW OFTEN DO YOU LIE? IF YOU ANSWER IS "HARDLY EVER," YOU'RE PROBABLY LYING RIGHT NOW. LYING IS MORE COMMON THAN YOU MIGHT THINK. MOST OF US LIE AT LEAST ONCE OR TWICE A DAY.

Why do I tell so many little lies?

Think of any conversation you had during the past week that lasted ten minutes or more: there's a one-in-five chance you lied during that conversation. During one week, you are likely to deceive nearly 33 percent of the people you interact with one-on-one.

Some relationships involve more lying than others. For example, university students have been found to lie to their mothers in half of all conversations. And it's worth pointing out social pleasantries like "I'm well, thanks" or "it's no problem" didn't count as lies in this research.

Lies are also common in romantic relationships. Eighty-five percent of university student couples said one or both partners had lied about past relationships. And dating couples lie in about a third of their interactions. But the lies we tell to the people closest to us are more likely to be discovered. It's also worth pointing out that while people in all cultures lie, we just lie about different things and in different ways.

LIAR, LIAR, PANTS ON FIRE

Like the boy who cried wolf, any parent will attest to the fact kids lie, and they start early. Research shows even six-month-olds will "fake cry" to get attention when nothing is wrong. And children learn to lie, both to protect

themselves and help others, from the age of two. At two, kids lie to deny wrongdoing and escape punishment: I didn't have any of the cake, says the kid with chocolate frosting all over her mouth. Two- and three-year-olds tend to be very unconvincing liars. When asked about their behavior, most will confess.

But by three, kids have also learned to tell "white" lies like thanking someone for a present they don't like or want. These are important social skills to learn, but learning to lie is a complex business. In order to lie, a child has to understand the fact that other people have their own separate, and potentially very different, thoughts. It is the process of learning to consider what other people think and feel that enables a child not only to lie, but lie convincingly. Even if you think you're good at picking up when your kid is lying to you, chances are you're not. Studies of more than 10,000 kids and adults found adults correctly identify lies less than half the time. That's right—you might as well flip a coin.

LIES, SWEET LITTLE LIES

We all lie to get what we want and avoid certain consequences. Lying is thought to be closely linked to self-esteem: as soon as we feel threatened, we're tempted to concoct bigger and more complicated lies to protect ourselves. More often though, the lies we tell to protect ourselves are only small. Small lies allow us to still believe we are fundamentally honest people. We tell lies when we are short on time and need to quickly cover up, but also if we simply feel justified in lying.

It turns out that rather than being deceiving two-faced fakes, a lot of the lies we tell are designed to help others. Many of our lies are the result of us pretending to like someone or something in order to protect someone else's feelings. These lies can be important parts of tact and politeness and as Jim Carrey showed us in Liar Liar, the world would definitely not be a happier place if we only ever told the absolute truth.

FROM LITTLE THINGS, BIG THINGS GROW

We start lying when we're very young. But why do most of us stick with garden-variety little lies, while others lie about big stuff? Research suggests compulsive liars effectively train their brains to ignore the guilty feelings most of us experience when we lie. If you don't feel guilty about lying, it's not at all difficult to lie again. Remember the amygdala—the part of our brain linked to fear, pleasure, and the "fight or flight" response? Brain scans of people encouraged to lie repeatedly showed that the response in the amygdala decreased with repeated lies. Our brains become desensitized to lying: the more we lie, the easier it is to lie again and again.

Presumably then, lying less often should make it harder to lie. And trying to lie less may well be a challenge we should all embrace: research shows telling the truth when we are tempted to lie can significantly improve our physical and mental health. And that's the truth.

Whether it's evading taxes, being unfaithful, doping in sports, making up data or committing financial fraud, deceivers often recall how small acts of dishonesty snowballed over time.

Tali Sharot, Professor of Cognitive Neuroscience, University College London

Why do I crave junk food late at night?

If you often find yourself craving junk food at night, you're not alone. Jawbone, the company behind a well-known fitness tracking device, recently released summary data about the food choices their users were making. Their findings were predictable. For example, people choose milk or yogurt rather than vegetables for breakfast. Consumption of vegetables peaks at dinnertime but drops dramatically after 8:00 p.m. At the same time, foods high in fats and sugars are strongly preferred between 8:00 p.m. and about 4:00 a.m.

This leads to an obvious question. Does being tired (which is likely if you are up in the small hours) cause people to crave fatty or sugary food? Many studies have shown a link between sleep deprivation and obesity, but that correlation doesn't tell us whether being short on sleep actually leads us to eat more junk food.

There have been many different explanations for the link between obesity and lack of sleep. For example, we know missing out on sleep disrupts the hormones that control our appetite. There's also the simple fact that the less time you spend sleeping, the more time you can spend eating. And if you aren't getting much sleep, it's likely you feel too tired to head to the gym. We also know drinking alcohol, which people are more likely to

do at night, leads to eating more. But is there a more direct link between being sleep-deprived and craving fast food?

OFF TO THE SLEEP LAB

Recent research specifically tested whether a person who is sleep-deprived eats more fatty and sugary snacks than when the same person has had enough sleep. Healthy volunteers aged between 18 and 30 each spent two four-day visits staying at a university lab. During both visits, the volunteers ate identical meals, at 9:00 a.m., 2:00 p.m., and 7:00 p.m. During one visit, they slept an average of seven and a half hours each night. But during the second stay, they weren't allowed to stay in bed for long and slept on average only four hours and 11 minutes per night. On the fourth night of each stay, the volunteers were offered a range of snacks.

When the study volunteers were sleep-deprived, they binged on fatty and sugary snacks (think candy, chips, and ice cream) and ate an average of 300 extra calories. Three hundred calories is way more than needed to compensate for the extra hours of being awake: you only need about 17 extra calories for each additional hour you are up and about. That's the equivalent of less than half an apple! But those who took part in the study said when they were sleep-deprived, they felt hungrier and found it very hard to resist the high-fat snacks on offer, even though there were healthy options available.

MARIJUANA MUNCHIES—WITHOUT THE MARIJUANA

The researchers analyzed the volunteers' blood to see if levels of particular appetite-related hormones could explain the increase in snacking. They also looked at levels of chemicals called endocannabinoids (named after cannabis, the plant that led to their discovery). The endocannabinoid system involves receptors in the body that affect the immune system and the

Our findings suggest that sleep deprivation makes our brain more susceptible to enticing food smells, so it might be worth taking a detour to avoid your local doughnut store next time you catch a 6:00 a.m. flight.

Thorsten Kahnt, Associate Professor of Neurology, Northwestern University

regulation of appetite hormones. And it's this system that is directly affected by marijuana, explaining the infamous "marijuana munchies."

When sleep-deprived, the volunteers had higher levels of a particular endocannabinoid called 2-AG that increase the pleasure we get from eating sugary, fatty foods. The daily rhythm of 2-AG was different: when the volunteers were low on sleep, the chemical remained at high levels in the body until about 9:00 p.m., rather than until 2:00 p.m., which is normal.

What does all that mean? Simply that when you're sleep-deprived, you crave fatty and sugary foods, and you get a lot of pleasure from eating them. It doesn't matter if you've just eaten a large dinner a few hours earlier; you're going to find it very hard to resist pizza, chocolate cookies, and ice cream.

Does it matter if you binge on junk food at night? If you're trying to lose weight, chomping cookies in the small hours is probably not ideal. But there's another reason to shut the fridge and go to bed. Research in mice suggests eating at a time you would normally be asleep may eventually lead to difficulties in both learning and in storing long-term memories.

About the author

DR. JEN MARTIN is an award-winning educator with a PhD from the University of Melbourne, Australia, where she founded and now leads the highly acclaimed Science Communication Teaching Program. She is deeply committed to helping scientists develop the skills they need to be visible, make connections, and have impact. She also writes the blog espressoscience.com and has a popular weekly radio segment—"Weird Science"—on Australia's largest independent radio station, Triple R. Jen was named the Unsung Hero of Australian Science Communication for 2019.

About the illustrator

HOLLY JOLLEY is a Chilean-British freelance illustrator and designer based in Santiago. She spends her days painting, reading, and drinking tea surrounded by her collection of books, glittery shoes, and flea market treasures. Her work ranges from editorial illustration to prints, brand collaborations, patterns, and art direction. The distinctive soft and quirky style of her artwork finds inspiration in nature, fashion, and daily life feelings.

Sources

The following research papers are referred to throughout the book.

SECTION 1 WHO AM I?

Why can't I remember my childhood?
• *The cognitive neuroscience of human memory since H.M.* Squire LR, & Wixted JT (2011) Annual Review of Neuroscience, 34:259–288.
• *Hippocampal Neurogenesis Regulates Forgetting During Adulthood and Infancy.* Akers KG, Martinez-Canabal A, Restiv L, Yiu AP, De Cristofaro A, Hsiang H, Wheeler AL, Guskjolen A, Niibori Y, Shoji H, Ohira K, Richards BA, Miyakawa T, Josselyn SA & Frankland PW (2014) Science 344(6184):598–602.
• *Engram cells retain memory under retrograde amnesia.* Ryan TJ, Roy DS, Pignatelli M, Arons A & Tonegawa S (2015) Science 348(6238):1007–1013.

Why do I cringe at teenage me?
• *The rank-order consistency of personality traits from childhood to old age: A quantitative review of longitudinal studies.* Roberts BW & DelVecchio WF (2000) Psychological Bulletin 126(1):3–25.
• *Development of personality in early and middle adulthood: Set like plaster or persistent change?* Srivastava S, John OP, Gosling SD & Potter J (2003) Journal of Personality and Social Psychology 84(5):1041–1053.
• *Personality stability from age 14 to age 77 years.* Harris MA, Brett CE, Johnson W & Deary IJ (2016) Psychology and Aging 31(8):862–874.

Why does my time pass so quickly?
• *Aging and the speed of time.* Friedman WJ & Janssen SM (2010) Acta Psychologica 134(2):130–141.
• *Why does life appear to speed up as people get older?* Janssen SMJ, Naka M & Friedman WJ (2013) Time & Society 22(2):274–290.
• *Whose Time Flies: Meaning in Life Influences Time Awareness.* Zheng X & Wang W (2020) Journal of Adult Development 27:249–257.

Why do I feel existential on some birthdays?
• *The post-birthday world: consequences of temporal landmarks for temporal self-appraisal and motivation.* Peetz J & Wilson AE (2013) Journal of Personality and Social Psychology 104(2):249–266.
• *The Fresh Start Effect: Temporal Landmarks Motivate Aspirational Behavior.* Dai H, Milkman KL & Riis J (2014) Management Science 60(10):2563–2582.
• *People search for meaning when they approach a new decade in chronological age.* Alter AL & Hershfield HE (2014) Proceedings of the National Academy of Sciences USA 111(48):17066–70.

Why do some smells make me homesick?
• *The Emotional Distinctiveness of Odor-evoked Memories.* Herz RS & Cupchik GC (1995) Chemical Senses 20(5):517–528.
• *Coordination of entorhinal–hippocampal ensemble activity during associative learning.* Igarashi K, Lu L, Colgin L, Moser M-B & Moser EI (2014) Nature 510(7503):143–147.
• *Hippocampal projections to the anterior olfactory nucleus differentially convey spatiotemporal information during episodic odour memory.* Aqrabawi AJ & Kim JC (2018) Nature Communications 9(1):2735.

Why does silence calm me?

• *Cardiovascular, cerebrovascular, and respiratory changes induced by different types of music in musicians and non-musicians: the importance of silence.* Bernardi L, Porta C & Sleight P (2006) Heart 92(4):445–452.

• *Is silence golden? Effects of auditory stimuli and their absence on adult hippocampal neurogenesis.* Kirste I, Nicola Z, Kronenberg G, Walker TL, Liu RC & Kempermann G (2015) Brain Structure and Function 220:1221–1228.

• *The Brain's Default Mode Network.* Raichle ME (2015) Annual Review of Neuroscience 38:433–447.

Why do horror movies give me a thrill?

• *Playing With Fear: A Field Study in Recreational Horror.* Andersen MM, Schjoedt U, Price H, Rosas E, Scrivner C & Clasen M (2020) Psychological Science 31(12):1497–1510.

• *Dissociable neural systems for unconditioned acute and sustained fear.* Hudson M, Seppälä K, Putkinen V, Sun L, Glerean E, Karjalainen T, Karlsson HK, Hirvonen J & Nummenmaa L (2020) NeuroImage 216:116522.

• *(Why) Do You Like Scary Movies? A Review of the Empirical Research on Psychological Responses to Horror Films.* Martin GN (2019) Frontiers in Psychology 10:2298.

Why do colors change my mood?

• *Can Uniform Color Color Aggression? Quasi-Experimental Evidence From Professional Ice Hockey.* Webster GD, Urland GR & Correll J (2012) Social Psychological and Personality Science 3(3):274–278.

• *Does green mean healthy? Nutrition label color affects perceptions of healthfulness.* Schuldt, JP (2013) Health Communication 28(8):814–821.

• *Meta-Analysis of the Effect of Red on Perceived Attractiveness.* Lehmann GK, Elliot AJ, Calin-Jageman RJ (2018) Evolutionary Psychology 16(4):1474704918802412.

Why do I hate doing absolutely nothing?

• *Just think: The challenges of the disengaged mind.* Wilson TD, Reinhard DA, Westgate EC, Gilbert DT, Ellerbeck N, Hahn C, Brown CL & Shaked A (2014) Science 345(6192):75–77.

• *With a little help for our thoughts: Making it easier to think for pleasure.* Westgate EC, Wilson TD & Gilbert DT (2017) Emotion 17(5):828–839.

• *Bored Into Depletion? Toward a Tentative Integration of Perceived Self-Control Exertion and Boredom as Guiding Signals for Goal-Directed Behavior.* Wolff W & Martarelli CS (2020) Perspectives on Psychological Science 15(5):1272–1283.

Why do I find baby animals so cute?

• *Baby schema modulates the brain reward system in nulliparous women.* Glocker ML, Langleben DD, Ruparel K, Loughead JW, Valdez JN, Griffin MD, Sachser N & Gur RC (2009) Proceedings of the National Academy of Sciences USA 106(22):9115–9.

• *Dimorphous expressions of positive emotion: displays of both care and aggression in response to cute stimuli.* Aragón OR, Clark MS, Dyer RL & Bargh JA (2015) Psychological Science 26(3):259–273.

• *The power of Kawaii: viewing cute images promotes a careful behavior and narrows attentional focus.* Nittono H, Fukushima M, Yano A & Moriya H (2012) PLoS One 7(9):e46362.

Why do I always feel like I'm missing out?

• *Motivational, emotional, and behavioral correlates of fear of missing out.* Przybylski AK, Murayama K, DeHaan CR & Gladwell V (2013) Computers in Human Behaviour 29(4):1841–1848.

• *Fear of Missing Out as a Predictor of Problematic Social Media Use and Phubbing Behavior among Flemish Adolescents.* Franchina V, Vanden Abeele M, van Rooij AJ, Lo Coco G & De Marez L (2018) International Journal of Environmental Research and Public Health 15(10):2319.

• *A threat to loyalty: Fear of missing out (FOMO) leads to reluctance to repeat current experiences.* Hayran C, Anik L & Gürhan-Canli Z (2020) PLoS One 15(4):e0232318.

Why do I feel like I'm being watched?

• *Humans have an expectation that gaze is directed toward them.* Mareschal I, Calder AJ & Clifford CW (2013) Current Biology 23(8): 717–721.

• *Amygdala activation for eye contact despite complete cortical blindness.* Burra N, Hervais-Adelman A, Kerzel D, Tamietto M, de Gelder B & Pegna AJ (2013) Journal of Neuroscience 33(25):10483–9.

• *Being watched: Effects of an audience on eye gaze and prosocial behaviour.* Cañigueral R & Hamilton AFC (2019) Acta Psychologica 195:50–63.

Why does everyone I know have more friends than me?

• *Coevolution of neocortical size, group size and language in humans.* Dunbar, R (1993) Behavioral and Brain Sciences 16(4):681–694.

• *Modeling users' activity on Twitter networks: validation of Dunbar's number.* Gonçalves B, Perra N & Vespignani A (2011) PLoS One 6(8):e22656.

• *Calling Dunbar's numbers.* Mac Carron P, Kaski K & Dunbar R (2016) Social Networks 47: 151–155.

Why do I feel like I'm going to be found out?

• *The Imposter Phenomenon in High Achieving Women: Dynamics and Therapeutic Intervention.* Clance PR & Imes S (1978) Psychotherapy Theory, Research and Practice 15:1–8.

• *Validation of the Impostor Phenomenon among Managers.* Rohrmann S, Bechtoldt MN & Leonhardt M (2016) Frontiers in Psychology 7:821.

• *Prevalence, Predictors, and Treatment of*

Impostor Syndrome: a Systematic Review. Bravata DM, Watts SA, Keefer AL, Madhusudhan DK, Taylor KT, Clark DM, Nelson RS, Cokley KO & Hagg HK (2020) Journal of General Internal Medicine 35(4):1252–1275.

Why am I not a master of anything?

• *The role of deliberate practice in the acquisition of expert performance.* Ericsson KA, Krampe RT & Tesch-Römer C (1993) Psychological Review 100(3):363–406.

• *Deliberate practice and performance in music, games, sports, education, and professions: a meta-analysis.* Macnamara BN, Hambrick DZ & Oswald FL (2014) Psychological Science 25(8):1608–1618.

• *The Relationship Between Deliberate Practice and Performance in Sports: A Meta-Analysis.* Macnamara BN, Moreau D & Hambrick DZ (2016) Perspectives on Psychological Science 11(3):333–350.

Why do I remember things that never happened?

• *Recent advances in false memory research.* Laney C & Loftus E (2013) South African Journal of Psychology 43(2):137–146.

• *Constructing rich false memories of committing crime.* Shaw J & Porter S (2015) Psychological Science 26(3):291–301.

• *Maladaptive Properties of Context-Impoverished Memories.* Zinn R, Leake J, Krasne FB, Corbit LH, Fanselow MS & Vissel B (2020) Current Biology 30:2300–2311.

SECTION 2 WHAT MAKES ME TICK?

Why do I keep pressing snooze?

• *Chronotype variation drives night-time sentinel-like behaviour in hunter-gatherers.* Samson DR, Crittenden AN, Mabulla IA, Mabulla AZP & Nunn CL (2017) Proceedings of the Royal Society of Biological Sciences 284(1858):20170967.

• Genome-wide association analyses of chronotype in 697,828 individuals provides insights into circadian rhythms. Jones SE, Lane JM, Wood AR, van Hees VT, Tyrrell J, Beaumont RN, Jeffries AR, Dashti HS, Hillsdon M, Ruth KS, Tuke MA, Yaghootkar H, Sharp SA, Jie Y, Thompson WD, Harrison JW, Dawes A, Byrne EM, Tiemeier H, Allebrandt KV, Bowden J, Ray DW, Freathy RM, Murray A, Mazzotti DR, Gehrman PR, Lawlor DA, Frayling TM, Rutter MK, Hinds DA, Saxena R & Weedon MN (2019) Nature Communications 10(1):343.

• Resetting the late timing of 'night owls' has a positive impact on mental health and performance. Facer-Childs ER, Middleton B, Skene DJ & Bagshaw AP (2019) Sleep Medicine 60:236–247.

Why can't I stop drinking coffee?

• Association of coffee drinking with total and cause-specific mortality. Freedman ND, Park Y, Abnet CC, Hollenbeck AR & Sinha R (2012) New England Journal of Medicine 366(20):1891–1904.

• Coffee consumption and health: umbrella review of meta-analyses of multiple health outcomes. Poole R, Kennedy OJ, Roderick P, Fallowfield JA, Hayes PC & Parkes J (2017) British Medical Journal 359:j5024.

• Post-study caffeine administration enhances memory consolidation in humans. Borota D, Murray E, Keceli G, Chang A, Watabe JM, Ly M, Toscano JP & Yassa MA (3024) Nature Neuroscience 17(2):201–203.

Why do I work better when I'm in the zone?

• The psychophysiology of flow during piano playing. de Manzano O, Theorell T, Harmat L & Ullén F (2010) Emotion 10(3):301–311.

• Neurocognitive mechanisms underlying the experience of flow. Dietrich A (2004) Conscious Cognition 13(4):746–761.

• The concept of flow. Nakamura J & Csikszentmihalyi M (2002) Handbook of Positive Psychology 89–105.

Why do I stick my tongue out when I'm concentrating?

• From mouth to hand: gesture, speech, and the evolution of right-handedness. Corballis MC (2003) Behavioral and Brain Sciences 26(2):199–220.

• Slip of the tongue: Implications for evolution and language development. Forrester GS & Rodriguez A (2015) Cognition 141:103–111.

• The human tongue show and observers' willingness to interact: replication and extensions. Jones N, Kearins J & Watson J (1987) Psychological Reports 60(3 Pt 1):759–764.

Why do I panic when I'm in the elevator?

• Near space and its relation to claustrophobic fear. Lourenco SF, Longo MR & Pathman T (2011) Cognition 119(3):448–453.

• A single gene defect causing claustrophobia. El-Kordi A, Kästner A, Grube S, Klugmann M, Begemann M, Sperling S, Hammerschmidt K, Hammer C, Stepniak B, Patzig J, de Monasterio-Schrader P, Strenzke N, Flügge G, Werner HB, Pawlak R, Nave KA & Ehrenreich H (2013) Translational Psychiatry 3(4):e254.

• The Effect of Augmented Reality and Virtual Reality on Inducing Anxiety for Exposure Therapy: A Comparison Using Heart Rate Variability. Tsai CF, Yeh SC, Huang Y, Wu Z, Cui J & Zheng L (2018) Journal of Healthcare Engineering: 6357351.

Why do I keep putting things off?

• The nature of procrastination: a meta-analytic and theoretical review of quintessential self-regulatory failure. Steel P (2007) Psychological Bulletin 133(1):65–94.

• I forgive myself: now I can study: How self-forgiveness for procrastinating can reduce future procrastination. Wohl MJA, Pychyl TA & Bennett SH (2010) Personality and Individual Differences 48(7):803–808.

• Procrastination as a Self-Regulation Failure:

The Role of Impulsivity and Intrusive Thoughts. Rebetez MML, Rochat L, Barsics C & Van der Linden M (2018) Psychological Reports 121(1):26–41.

Why can't I multitask?

• *A comparison of the cell phone driver and the drunk driver.* Strayer DL, Drews FA & Crouch DJ (2006) Human Factors 48(2):381–391.

• *Supertaskers: Profiles in extraordinary multitasking ability.* Watson JM & Strayer DL (2010) Psychonomic Bulletin & Review 17(4):479–485.

• *Higher media multitasking activity is associated with smaller gray-matter density in the anterior cingulate cortex.* Loh KK & Kanai R (2014) PLoS One 9(9):e106698.

Why don't I remember why I walked into this room?

• *Walking through doorways causes forgetting: Further explorations.* Radvansky GA, Krawietz SA & Tamplin AK (2011) Quarterly Journal of Experimental Psychology 64(8):1632–45.

• *Walking through doorways causes forgetting: Younger and older adults.* Radvansky GA, Pettijohn KA & Kim J (2015) Psychological Aging 30(2):259–265.

• *Mentally walking through doorways causes forgetting: The location updating effect and imagination.* Lawrence Z & Peterson D (2016) Memory 24(1):12–20.

Why do I blink so much?

• *Synchronization of spontaneous eyeblinks while viewing video stories.* Nakano T, Yamamoto Y, Kitajo K, Takahashi T & Kitazawa S (2009) Proceedings of the Royal Society B Biological Sciences 276(1673):3635–44.

• *Blink and you'll miss it: the role of blinking in the perception of magic tricks.* Wiseman RJ & Nakano T (2016) PeerJ 4:e1873.

• *Medial prefrontal cortex supports perceptual memory.* Schwiedrzik CM, Sudmann SS, Thesen T,

Wang X, Groppe DM, Mégevand P, Doyle W, Mehta AD, Devinsky O & Melloni L (2018) Current Biology 28(18):R1094–R1095.

Why do I blush?

• *I blush, therefore I will be judged negatively: influence of false blush feedback on anticipated others' judgments and facial coloration in high and low blushing-fearfuls.* Dijk C, Voncken MJ & de Jong PJ (2009) Behavioral Research Therapy 47(7):541–547.

• *The remedial value of blushing in the context of transgressions and mishaps.* Dijk C, de Jong PJ & Peters ML (2009) Emotion 9(2):287–291.

• *Intrapersonal and interpersonal concomitants of facial blushing during everyday social encounters.* aan het Rot M, Moskowitz DS & de Jong PJ (2015) PLoS One 10(2):e0118243.

Why is holding eye contact so exhausting?

• *Averting the gaze disengages the environment and facilitates remembering.* Glenberg AM, Schroeder JL & Robertson DA (1998) Memory Cognition 26(4):651–658.

• *Pupil dilation as an index of preferred mutual gaze duration.* Binetti N, Harrison C, Coutrot A, Johnston A & Mareschal I (2016) Royal Society Open Science 3(7):160086.

• *When we cannot speak: Eye contact disrupts resources available to cognitive control processes during verb generation.* Kajimura S & Nomura M (2016) Cognition 157:352–357.

Why can't I stop humming that song?

• *Music in everymind: Commonality of involuntary musical imagery.* Liikkanen LA (2008) Proceedings of the 10th International Conference on Music Perception and Cognition, Japan.

• *How do "earworms" start? Classifying the everyday circumstances of Involuntary Musical Imagery.* Williamson VJ, Jilka SR, Fry J, Finkel S, Müllensiefen D & Stewart L (2012) Psychology of Music 40(3):259–284.

• *Sticky Tunes: How Do People React to Involuntary Musical Imagery?* Williamson VJ, Liikkanen LA, Jakubowski K & Stewart L (2014) PLoS ONE 9(1):e86170.

Why do I see faces in everyday objects?
• *The potato chip really does look like Elvis! Neural hallmarks of conceptual processing associated with finding novel shapes subjectively meaningful.* Voss JL, Federmeier KD & Paller KA (2012) Cerebral Cortex 22(10):2354–2364.
• *Seeing Jesus in toast: neural and behavioral correlates of face pareidolia.* Liu J, Li J, Feng L, Li L, Tian J & Lee K (2014) Cortex 53:60–77.
• *Face Pareidolia Recruits Mechanisms for Detecting Human Social Attention.* Palmer CJ & Clifford CWG (2020) Psychological Science 31(8):1001–1012.

Why do I take so many photos?
• *Point-and-shoot memories: the influence of taking photos on memory for a museum tour.* Henkel LA (2014) Psychological Science 25(2):396–402.
• *Media usage diminished memory for experiences.* Tamir DI, Templeton EM, Ward AF & Zaki J (2018) Journal of Experimental Social Psychology 76:161–168.
• *Forget in a flash: A Further Investigation of the Photo-Taking-Impairment Effect.* Soares JS & Storm BC (2018) Journal of Applied Research in Memory and Cognition 7(1):154–160.

Why do I like doodling?
• *Doodling and the default network of the brain.* Schott GD (2011) Lancet 378(9797):1133–1134.
• *Drawing pictures during learning from scientific text: testing the generative drawing effect and the prognostic drawing effect.* Schmeck A, Mayer RE, Opfermann M, Pfeiffer V & Leutner D (2014) Contemporary Educational Psychology 39(4):275–286.
• *The drawing effect: Evidence for reliable and robust memory benefits in free recall.* Wammes JD, Meade ME & Fernandes MA (2016) Quarterly Journal of Experimental Psychology 69(9):1752–1776.

Why do I tell so many little lies?
• *Lying in everyday life.* DePaulo BM, Kashy DA, Kirkendol SE, Wyer MM, Epstein JA (1996) Journal of Personality and Social Psychology 70(5):979–995.
• *Honesty requires time (and lack of justifications).* Shalvi S, Eldar O & Bereby-Meyer Y (2012) Psychological Science 23(10):1264–1270.
• *The brain adapts to dishonesty.* Garrett N, Lazzaro SC, Ariely D & Sharot T (2016) Nature Neuroscience 19(12):1727–1732.

Why do I crave junk food at night?
• *The internal circadian clock increases hunger and appetite in the evening independent of food intake and other behaviors.* Scheer FA, Morris CJ & Shea SA (2013) Obesity 21(3):421–423.
• *The endocannabinoid system controls food intake via olfactory processes.* Soria-Gómez E, Bellocchio L, Reguero L, Lepousez G, Martin C, Bendahmane M, Ruehle S, Remmers F, Desprez T, Matias I, Wiesner T, Cannich A, Nissant A, Wadleigh A, Pape HC, Chiarlone AP, Quarta C, Verrier D, Vincent P, Massa F, Lutz B, Guzmán M, Gurden H, Ferreira G, Lledo PM, Grandes P & Marsicano G (2014) Nature Neuroscience 17(3):407–415.
• *Sleep Restriction Enhances the Daily Rhythm of Circulating Levels of Endocannabinoid 2-Arachidonoylglycerol.* Hanlon EC, Tasali E, Leproult R, Stuhr KL, Doncheck E, de Wit H, Hillard CJ & Van Cauter E (2016) Sleep 39(3):653–664.

Index

For Euan, Rohan & Kirri

First Published in North America by
Princeton Architectural Press
70 West 36th Street
New York, NY 10018
www.papress.com

Copyright © Elwin Street Limited 2022
Illustrations © Holly Jolley

Conceived and produced by
Elwin Street Productions
10 Elwin Street
London E2 7BU

Printed and bound in China
25 24 23 22   4 3 2 1 First edition

ISBN 978-1-64896-173-1
Library of Congress Control Number: 2022931442

For Princeton Architectural Press:
Editors: Rob Shaeffer, Stephanie Holstein
Cover Design: Paul Wagner

If you feel affected by any of the issues discussed in this book, these resources offer support and information:

Child Mind Institute: childmind.org
Mental Health America: www.mhanational.org
National Institute of Mental Health: www.nimh.nih.gov